D0992843

Simply Love

# Simply Love: Catholic Marriage Day by Day

Troy and Kathleen Billings

Our Sunday Visitor
Huntington, Indiana

Our Sunday Visitor Publishing Division
Our Sunday Visitor, Inc.
200 Noll Plaza
Huntington, IN 46750
1-800-348-2440

ISBN: 978-1-68192-423-6 (Inventory No. T2315)
1. RELIGION—Christian Life—Love & Marriage.
2.RELIGION—Christian Life—Devotional.
3.RELIGION—Christianity—Catholic.

eISBN: 978-1-68192-424-3
LCCN: 2022945026

Cover and interior design: Chelsea Alt
Cover art: AdobeStock

PRINTED IN THE UNITED STATES OF AMERICA

*In heartfelt gratitude for our five beautiful children —*
*Joseph, Gemma, David, Marianna, and Anthony —*
*who inspire us daily to love deeper and to live fully*
*the vows we professed on our wedding day*

# Introduction

## *Taking One for the Team*

We have a tradition we began a few years into our marriage that has helped us stay focused on God's will for us as a couple and keep a clear vision of our mutual goals and aspirations. At the beginning of each new year, we have a date night where we set goals for our marriage and come up with a game plan for the new year ahead.

Marriage goals aren't like setting a goal for reading more books or lifting more weight. They can't reflect just one person's priorities. They must be shared aspirations — and that is why praying together is so very important.

From day one, Troy has referred to the two of us as a team. If a team wants to win, each player has to work together toward that goal. In marriage, our ultimate goal is to get each other to heaven. Still, we think most couples would agree that having a fulfilling, happy marriage would be considered a *win* on this side of heaven! Sometimes though, we get knocked down and forget that we are on the same team. That, too, is why finding a way to pray together is important.

Teammates are accountable to one another. If one teammate is in the wrong, it affects the entire team. It is the same in marriage. It is important to forgive, but also to hold each other accountable. Of course, there is a difference between holding a grudge and holding your spouse accountable for a wrong that needs to be made right. If we want a successful marital team, both of us need to admit it when we are wrong. The habit of praying together makes asking for and granting forgiveness easier, and holding onto anger and resentment more difficult.

In a team, when one player is down, another player steps up to the plate to fill in. Again, it is the same in marriage. When one of us is down, is the other lovingly and emotionally supportive, helping to pick them up? Or do we ignore the fact that they are down? Our own wounds, pride, or lack of energy may make it difficult to help when one of us is in a down time, but God calls us to uphold each other. Praying together helps us balance our strengths and needs, and teaches us how to accept our limitations and rely on God's grace.

Coming into God's presence together briefly but *daily* reinforces the fact that you are on the same team. (After all, it was God who brought you together in the first place!) But many couples — even couples who are deeply committed to their faith — struggle to find a time, a place, or a way to pray together that works for them. Schedules can be hectic, and space may be at a premium. But more often, difficulties arise because prayer is such a personal and intimate endeavor. One person has a strong devotion to the Rosary and the other doesn't. One loves silent meditation and the other prefers music. One is comfortable speaking to God in their own words, and the other treasures traditional prayers that have been offered over the centuries.

In the daily reflections that follow, we have included a broad range of practical tools as well as things to think and pray about. Our greater purpose, however, is to provide you with a resource you can share — one that will help you establish a habit of coming to God *together*, as a couple, seeking his grace to live your marriage as the beautiful vocation it is. We know that the daily habit of praying together will bring joy and strength to your marriage, because we have experienced this in our own.

We don't think that fantasy romance has anything on real-life love. Marriage is romantic, fun, and exciting; it is also demanding, exhausting, and downright hard. This book is the product of our life experience and our ongoing reflection on both our successes and failures in relationships. On a personal level, God allowed us both to experience the deep pain of being in a lifeless first marriage, going through the annulment process, and then remarrying each other in the Church. When we married in 2006, we were deeply convicted that God would use what he allowed us to go through to someday help other couples.

While we both began our marriage with full knowledge of the beauty of the Sacrament of Matrimony and wisdom gained from the pain of the past, with a deep desire to use our collective experiences as a springboard to help Catholic married couples, we still had baggage we brought to the table. Our knowledge of God's plan for sacramental marriage was our foundation, but we had to learn how to put it into practice. Living the sacrament day in and day out with a fierce commitment to chiseling away our selfish tendencies, working through our differences, and focusing our efforts on moving forward in God's plan for our marriage without allowing the past to dictate our future, we have discovered the deep, authentic joy that comes from choosing to "simply love" one day at a time.

In this book, we begin each day's entry with wisdom drawn from a saint or from the Scriptures. These quotes are intended to give you a springboard for the reflection that follows. We've chosen not to date these reflections to allow you more freedom to decide when you begin. (Consider making Day 1 your wedding anniversary, the New Year, or to mark the beginning or end of a time of transition.) We also hope that simply numbering the days will help you not to worry about missing an occasional day or two along the way. If you do, just pick up where you left off!

Above all, we want to encourage you. Whatever your marriage is like today, there is always more God wants to give you. He has a unique plan for each one of us and for every married couple. Yet every one of those plans has one thing in common: God's desire to draw you closer to himself and to each other. The purpose of this book is to give you a vehicle for growing in spiritual intimacy with each other and with God — in less than five minutes a day.

# DAY 1

*Make few resolutions. Make specific resolutions.*
*And fulfill them with the help of God.*

— *St. Josemaría Escrivá*

We set goals at work to increase our numbers or productivity. We set personal goals to improve our health or achieve something important to us. We set communal goals to work toward a common purpose. And we set financial goals to be more financially solvent. So why not set goals for our marriage as well? Setting goals as a couple helps to fortify our relationship by working together toward a common purpose.

Remember that your primary goal is to get each other to heaven. Everything else is secondary. So, it's important to be flexible and take time to reevaluate your more immediate goals periodically. Celebrate your accomplishments along the way and redesign your plan if necessary. Life happens, and inevitably something will cause you to temporarily get off track. The important thing is to get back on track as soon as possible and make adjustments to goals if a curve ball is thrown your way. Clearcut goals, focus, and determination certainly help. But an openness to God's grace, especially the sacramental grace of marriage, makes all things possible!

**Prayer:** Lord, guide us as we strive to set worthy and realistic goals for our marriage. Amen.

# Day 2

*I'm always so happy with him, he makes my life very pleasant. What a holy man my husband is. I wish the same for all women; that's my wish for them for the New Year.*

— *St. Zélie Martin*

We all want to be so happy and content in our marriage that we would wish others could experience the same joy and fulfillment we do. This *is* what God desires for us! God wants Christian husbands to be men their wives are proud of, to be so close to Jesus that they reflect him to all, especially their wives. And God wants Christian wives to not only see his goodness in the men who love them, but also draw God's goodness out through their unconditional love and respect for their husbands. God hungers for us to be happily married. He is our Father, and he wants his children to flourish and be joyful. When a husband and wife love God and work together in union with the Holy Spirit, amazing things can and do happen. Despite whatever life may throw at us, there is an underlying unity in our marriage that brings joy in tackling the everyday together, trusting in God's providence as a couple. God's design for marriage is that we become saints together.

**Prayer:** Lord, please help us cultivate the kind of love in our marriage that saints are made of. Sts. Louis and Zélie Martin, pray for us!

# Day 3

*Do something beautiful for God. Do it with your life.*
*Do it every day. Do it in your own way. But do it!*

— *St. Teresa of Calcutta*

Think of the above quote as a short motivational speech by Mother Teresa as you begin today's reflection. What is one consistent thing you can do this year for your marriage? If that is kissing your spouse goodnight every night, then do it. If that is making your spouse coffee every morning, then do it. If that is committing to a monthly date night, then do it. (Hint: Praying together every day is a good answer, too.) God doesn't really care how grand or how small the beauty you offer him is. He only cares that you keep moving forward, that you keep creating something beautiful for him in your own unique way, and that you do it with all your heart. Whatever you do out of love for your spouse, you do for God, and in his eyes it is beautiful!

**Prayer:** Lord, we pray that our love for one another may be a continual gift of beauty to you. Amen.

# Day 4

*As to the past, let us entrust it to God's mercy, the future to Divine Providence. Our task is to live holy the present moment.*

— *St. Gianna Beretta Molla*

Troy has a natural gift for living in the present moment. He knows how to enjoy life and live it well. Kathleen, on the other hand, fights the inclination to worry about the effects of the past on the present. Understanding this difference in our makeup has facilitated our understanding of one another in the way we each respond to the past, live in the present, and view the future.

Aside from our unique personal gifts and preferences, we also bring the gifts of our femininity and masculinity to our marriage. In this we discover equilibrium. Our unique gifts and perspectives as male and female complement one another and assist us in giving the past to God, trusting his plan for the future, and being able to wholly live our marriage in the present moment.

Troy's spreadsheets and Kathleen's to-do lists assist us in ordering our lives. That, in turn, provides us with a greater capacity to embrace the present moment and be at peace about our future. As a couple we plan, and we have a plan. But ultimately, we trust that God is in control.

**Prayer:** Lord, we entrust our past to your mercy and our future to your Divine Providence. Help us to live wholly in the present moment. Amen.

# Day 5

*Take heed to the path of your feet, then*
*all your ways will be sure.*

*— Proverbs 4:26*

If we are mindful of the path of our feet and diligent about leading our marriage in the right direction, we can be confident that God will honor and bless our lives together. At the beginning of each day, ideally together (although that's not always possible), we take a few minutes to discuss our agenda for the day and then present it before God in prayer. We ask him to bless our day, and we pray that we do his will and not our own. This sets our feet on the right path from the start of the day. Life happens, however, and inevitably there are days we fail to do this. That's OK. Once we recognize that we have not set out on the right course, we can stop and ask God to get us back on track. Heaven is our goal, and it is our duty as spouses to lead one other on the path to eternal life.

**Prayer:** Lord, please lead our marriage each day on the path that is directed toward heaven and eternal life with you. Amen.

# Day 6

*Man can fully discover his true self only
in a sincere giving of himself.*

— *Pope St. John Paul II*

If you aspire to build a successful marriage rather than become another negative statistic, take to heart these powerful words by one of the greatest saints of recent years. The very purpose and meaning of your life can only be understood in light of fully giving yourself to others. Marriage provides the perfect opportunity to discover why God created you. Every day there are opportunities to give yourself to your spouse and to die to yourself for your spouse. There are countless means, large and small, by which we can give ourselves — not just *of* ourselves — in marriage. To perform tasks for our spouse is one thing, but to perform those same tasks sincerely with a servant's heart is what differentiates a good marriage from a great marriage.

**Prayer:** Lord, help us to be a sincere gift to one another and fully discover our authentic purpose in life. Amen.

# DAY 7

*You know well that Our Lord does not look so much at the greatness of our actions, nor even at their difficulty, as at the love with which we do them.*

— *St. Thérèse of Lisieux*

Marriage is made up of many small things, and engaging in those small things with great love is our path to heaven. Pouring love into the mundane and messiness of everyday marital life is the nuts and bolts of a strong and healthy marriage.

The two of us frequently lift weights as a method to stay physically fit. The stronger our muscles become, the healthier we become, and the heavier the weight we are able to lift. To build strong muscles requires commitment and consistent effort. Of course, we didn't start with the heaviest weights, but the lightest. Marriage is a lot like weightlifting. Each small act done in love strengthens our marriage and burns away selfishness, and each wasted opportunity to love well through our daily actions weakens our marriage. A strong and fit marriage grows when small acts are done with great love.

**Prayer:** Lord, draw our attention to the small things and give us the necessary strength and stamina to pour love into all we do for each other. Amen.

# Day 8

*And that Christ may dwell in your hearts through faith; as you are being rooted and grounded in love.*

— *Ephesians 3:17*

We are both avid gardeners. We have a small vineyard, several fruit trees, and a huge vegetable and herb garden. There is a unique thrill that comes from witnessing something you plant grow and blossom. All living things thrive best when properly tended to in a healthy environment. Likewise, a marriage given fertile soil to grow in is more likely to flourish. Fertile soil provides a haven where authentic love can thrive. It is cultivated through each act of genuine love. Sacrifice for your spouse, listen to them, strive to meet their needs, praise them, encourage them, and pray for them. When your spouse fails, practice patience and generously forgive so they are free to truly express themselves without fear of judgment. If you root your marriage in God's love, it will be strong and capable of weathering the fluctuating seasons of life together.

**Prayer:** Lord, may our home be a seedbed of faith for your love to grow so our marriage can richly blossom. Amen.

# DAY 9

*Sanctify them in the truth; your word is truth.*

*— John 17:17*

Trust is the foundation of every relationship. This is especially true when it comes to building a healthy marriage. You cannot build a solid marriage on unstable ground. Yet it isn't hard to justify lying. We tell ourselves it's harmless or small, that it really doesn't matter. But dishonesty creates insecurity, suspicion, and doubt; it violates the trust marriage needs. Deceit can occur with words and with silence, but either way, falsehood prevents genuine intimacy. Withholding pertinent information from our spouse is just another form of lying. And the more often we are dishonest, the easier it becomes to lie — and the more difficult it becomes to tell the truth.

Are you always honest with your spouse? The truth might hurt or reveal some disagreement, but withholding the truth guarantees far more pain and damage in the long run. Once trust has been broken, there is no fast track to earning it back. God calls us to speak the truth and live with integrity.

**Prayer:** Lord, we trust you and we ask you to help us trust one another. May we always speak truth to one another. Amen.

# DAY 10

*The world offers you comfort, but you were not*
*made for comfort. You were made for greatness.*

— *Pope Benedict XVI*

We can get so downright cozy in our own little comfort zone that we become stagnant. Comfort is why so many of us never really test the waters beyond our own little bubble to see what more God is asking of us — or offering to us. But comfort will never really be enough, because we were made for greatness! Greatness grows through stepping out in faith even when that makes us uncomfortable.

In the middle of the COVID-19 pandemic, we left our comfortable home of fifteen years in Illinois to move to South Carolina. It was a calling God placed on our hearts — one we are immensely thankful we embraced. It was difficult to uproot our family, leave behind amazing friends and family, and plant our roots in a completely new location. But now we can clearly see that our move brought us exactly where God wanted us to be.

**Prayer:** Lord, give us the grace to say yes to your will, and help us to have the courage to leave our comfort zone to serve you and one another. Amen.

# DAY 11

*Do not try to excuse your faults; try to correct them.*

*— St. John Bosco*

None of us is perfect, and all of us have faults. In most cases, nobody knows our faults better than our spouse. That can make it difficult to continually grow in love for one another. One of the biggest threats to peace in our marriage is the inability to recognize when we have done something wrong. While sinful actions and negative reactions may be the result of an underlying circumstance that is outside our control, this does not give any of us permission to justify hurtful behavior. But even when we recognize a fault or failing, we can be tempted to give up on ourselves or one another by living in a way that accommodates or excuses faults rather than trying to correct them. Don't fall into this trap. Rather, sincerely apologize and make yourself accountable. Then pray for the grace to help each other, not with excuses, but with forgiveness and loving support.

**Prayer:** Lord, help us to be honest, accountable, and forthright with our shortcomings. Give us the grace to correct our faults. Amen.

# Day 12

*As iron is fashioned by the fire and on an anvil, so in the
fire of suffering and under the weight of trials, our souls
receive the form that Our Lord desires for them to have.*

— *St. Madeline Sophie Barat*

Life isn't easy, and marriage doesn't necessarily make it any easier. But we don't have to be afraid or try to avoid the inevitable challenges that being married presents. We find some of our greatest joys in one another, but also some of our greatest trials.

We have learned that it's best to meet our conflicts head on rather than sugarcoating an obvious problem or denying an elephant in the room. Love between spouses grows broader and deeper when we pass through the trials of married life with open and honest hearts. This demands the love and self-control to value the other person more than we value our own opinions, preferences, or being right. Like iron fashioned in fire, so too is our spousal love perfected through the day-to-day fires we pass through together as a married couple. Our marriage is continually molded into the form of unity Our Lord desires.

**Prayer:** Lord, help us be like clay in your hands as you mold us as a couple into the form you desire for our marriage. Amen.

# DAY 13

*We need to pray that married couples will love their
vocation, even when the road becomes difficult.*

— *Pope St. John Paul II*

It is precisely when the road becomes difficult in marriage that we are
presented with the opportunity to put into action, in the most authentic way, the vows we took on our wedding day. If it was not for the love
of our vocation, and our understanding of what we were committing to
on the day we entered our nuptial union, we might have thrown in the
towel a long time ago.

When the roads of married life become rough and the terrain difficult, we need to look past our problems and focus our gaze on Jesus.
Although we must do our part to resolve problems as we are able, if we
concentrate solely on the burden of the difficulty and how we can "fix it"
with our talents and resources, we are missing out on the most beautiful
dimensions of our vocation. Instead, we are called to tap into the grace of
the sacrament that flows from Christ through the Church.

**Prayer:** Lord, help us love our vocation, especially when our way becomes painful and difficult. May our love and understanding of our
commitment to one another be the glue that holds us together. Amen.

# DAY 14

*It is one thing to be conscious that the value of sex is a part*
*of all the rich storehouse of values with which the female*
*appears to the man. It is another to 'reduce' all the personal*
*riches of femininity to that single value, that is, of sex, as*
*a suitable object for the gratification of sexuality itself.*

— *Pope St. John Paul II (Theology of the Body)*

You should be physically attracted to your spouse. But sexual passion was never meant to be the foundation for marriage, but rather a gift given to married couples. Authentic sexual expression has two dimensions: unitive and procreative. The unitive aspect is the fulfillment of the one flesh union within the context of marriage, and the procreative is the couple's openness to life. If either aspect is ever removed from the sexual act, intimacy becomes disordered. This often makes couples feel they are no longer compatible, when in reality it is the disorder in their conjugal love revealing itself. Sexual intimacy is a means of giving ourselves completely. If it becomes more about receiving or even taking the other, we are falling short of the glory of marriage as God intended it.

**Prayer:** Lord, may the sexual expression of our conjugal love always be properly ordered. Amen.

# Day 15

*The glory of God is man fully alive.*

— *St. Irenaeus of Lyons*

One of our favorite things to do as a couple is to sit by a fire and cuddle. There is something incredibly mesmerizing about a fire — it draws you in. If you have ever tried to start a fire, you know it takes persistent effort and patience. Once the fire is going, it can usually sustain itself for a short while, but eventually you need to add more wood to keep the flames burning. If you allow the fire to die, it is a lot of work to get it going again. Maintaining the original flame is far easier than restarting the entire fire. It is the same in marriage.

As much as we both desire a holy marriage, it is easy for us to get sidetracked by the distractions of a busy family of seven. Perhaps the flame which initially ignited your marriage is still burning brightly, maybe it's on low flame, or perhaps the fire has completely gone out. Christ is the fire-starter and his presence in your marriage will fan the flames of your love. Make sure he is an invited guest in your home at all times.

**Prayer:** Lord, please help us keep the fire of our love, united in you, burning brightly. Amen.

# DAY 16

*Our business is to attain heaven; everything
else is a sheer waste of time.*

— *St. Vincent de Paul*

When we first married, we enthusiastically discussed all the "holy things" we would do to help one another get to heaven, and we naively believed that engaging in these spiritual practices was our ticket in. It wasn't long before we realized that holiness consists in embracing one another's faults and carrying one another's crosses. This is not to say that we should not also do "holy things," such as praying the Rosary or reading Sacred Scripture together. But we build our spiritual muscles and advance on our path to heaven together primarily by loving when it is difficult to love, forgiving when it is difficult to forgive, and swallowing our pride when we would rather toot our own horn. Prayer is the glue that keeps us united, and Mass is the pinnacle of our prayer life. Spiritual practices can assist us in living lives of virtue, but it is the everyday striving for heaven within our vocation of marriage that advances us on our path.

**Prayer:** Lord, give us the grace to distinguish being holy from simply doing holy things. May our love for one another and you be pure and authentic. Amen.

# Day 17

*The purpose of marriage is to help married people sanctify*
*themselves and others. For this reason, they receive a*
*special grace in the sacrament which Jesus Christ instituted.*
*Those who are called to the married state will, with the*
*grace of God, find within their state everything they need*
*to be holy, to identify themselves each day more with Jesus*
*Christ, and to lead those with whom they live to God.*

— *St. Josemaría Escrivá*

In marriage, sacramental grace is our number one resource. But if we do not ask God for the graces given to us by way of sacramental union, or if we fail to cooperate with them, they cannot help us. Our life as a married couple becomes holy only to the extent that we cooperate with God and allow him to work in and through us in our relationship. At the start of each day, then, ask God to equip you with the grace necessary to be a good husband or wife that day. This grace is our fuel to live the vocation of marriage in a way that is aligned with God's will and a sign of God's love for his Church.

**Prayer:** Lord, we ask for the grace necessary to live our sacramental life each day in line with your divine purpose for our marriage. May the grace of our sacrament freely flow between us as we love one another, and beyond us to all we meet. Amen.

# Day 18

*The proof of love is in the works. Where love exists, it works
great things. But when it ceases to act, it ceases to exist.*

— *St. Gregory the Great*

In 2019 Troy spent a great deal of time in Costa Rica working with a
client. Although he speaks Spanish fluently, he needed to bring himself
up to speed on technical terms in order to complete the project entirely
in the Spanish language. If he had not taken time to brush up his skills,
it would have been much more challenging to communicate effectively.
Something like this exists in marriage. Our spouse has a specific "love
language," a way in which he or she communicates and receives love.
When we learn that language and then speak it, our husband or wife feels
loved. If we do not learn to speak our spouse's love language fluently, then
our spouse may never fully receive our love for them in way that speaks
to their heart. Learning what language speaks love most deeply to your
spouse and committing yourself to speaking it, can strengthen the health
of your marriage.

**Prayer:** Lord, please give us the necessary grace to love our spouse in the
way they feel most loved. Amen.

# Day 19

*If you are wise therefore you will show yourself a
reservoir and not a canal. For a canal pours out as fast
as it takes in; but a reservoir waits till it is full before
it overflows, and so communicates a surplus.*

— *St. Bernard of Clairvaux*

To be a source of God's divine grace in our marriage, it is better to be a reservoir than a canal. That way, the grace of God can pour out of us from its abundance. It is essential to make time for rest, reflection, and prayer in order to love, honor, and cherish each other. Most of us are more like a canal than a reservoir. We dispense words as soon as they come into our minds and often take action without much thought, rather than allowing both our words and deeds to flow from a place of grace. When we know we are operating on a near-empty tank, it is even more important to be filled with God's never-ending grace. Then we can become a reservoir of his goodness from which our family — and especially our spouse — can continually draw.

**Prayer:** Lord, may we take the necessary time for rest, reflection, and prayer in order to continually fuel our souls with your grace. Amen.

# DAY 20

*Put up willingly with the faults of others if*
*you wish others to put up with yours.*

— *St. John Bosco*

A few weeks into our marriage, an older married man suggest that Troy always say, "Yes, dear," to Kathleen, regardless of how he really felt. If he just followed these words of wisdom, his friend promised, we would indeed have a happy marriage. Although his advice was followed by a chuckle, we knew he meant what he said, but it did not sit right with Kathleen. She didn't want her husband suppressing his real feelings in order to keep the peace. We all have faults, and the sooner we learn to manage them in our marriage, the happier and healthier we will be. "Yes, dear" is fine when it's genuine. But if it is said to avoid dealing with a fault or difficult situation, then we are being insincere, and our dishonesty in the present moment will eventually lead to an unpleasant resurfacing of emotion down the road. Likewise, it is wrong to expect our spouse to be patient with our shortcomings if we are not willing to offer the same courtesy.

**Prayer:** Lord, please help us practice patience when dealing with one another's faults — the same patience we would hope to receive. Amen.

# Day 21

*Put on then, as God's chosen ones, holy and beloved,
compassion, kindness, lowliness, meekness and
patience, forbearing one another and, if one has a
complaint against another, forgiving each other; as the
Lord has forgiven you, so you also must forgive.*

— *Colossians 3:12–13*

Our actions, both good and bad, can have long-lasting and even eternal consequences. The fragrance of our deeds — of how we treat each other — hangs in the air between us. Unfortunately, it is often easier for us to recall an incidence of how our spouse wronged us than it is to remember a kind or loving gesture. The minute we are hurt by our husband or wife, we are quick to remember previous injuries or injustices we have endured. Pain lingers, sometimes for a long period of time, depending on how deep the wound is. But it is sinful to bring up a past hurt that we have already forgiven. When we forgive, we must also let go and allow God to heal us. We must also do what we can to hold on to all that is good between us and not let our worst moments overshadow our best ones.

**Prayer:** Lord, help us focus on good that lingers and let go of any residual hurt or resentment we may feel over past wounds. Amen.

# Day 22

*The gift of grace increases as the struggle increases.*

— *St. Rose of Lima*

God often permits circumstances in our lives that involve substantial struggle. Yet there is comfort in knowing that if God in his wisdom allows the struggle, he will equip us with his strength. His plan is perfect, and when we trust in him, we have the mental stamina to endure whatever crosses he allows. God's grace is always more than sufficient for the struggle. Journeying through challenging seasons in union with God's grace helps to form your marriage. If you want to gain a great marriage, it is important to allow the Lord to mold it through the difficulties you encounter together. But don't try to do that on your own power! Rely on his strength to carry you and his love to comfort you. God will make use of the crosses he asks you to carry to prepare you for the mission he brought you together to accomplish.

**Prayer:** Lord, as we encounter various struggles as a married couple, please equip us with your grace to make good use of all we encounter for our growth and your glory. Amen.

# Day 23

*Truth suffers, but never dies.*

*— St. Teresa of Ávila*

Intimacy means to make our innermost self known. It is the act of connecting with our spouse so deeply that we understand one another, we value one another, and we trust one another. We all long for someone to know the "innermost" truth of who we are. This is the vulnerability that makes it possible for us to feel loved. If we are not intentional about it, we can easily become blind to the innermost truth of one another. Perhaps you are reticent to go there for fear of what you might discover or how that might make you more accountable. Go there anyway. Maybe you are reluctant to intimately share yourself for fear of being rejected. Share yourself anyway. Honesty is a form of intimacy. Our innermost truth does not die, but when spouses are unable to share that truth with each other, it suffers. Real growth comes in marriage when we are completely open with our spouse.

**Prayer:** Lord, help us to always be honest with one another and give us the grace to embrace the beauty of intimacy in our marriage. Amen.

# DAY 24

*There is nothing better or more necessary than love.*

— *St. John of the Cross*

Early on in our marriage, we both discovered the importance and value of couple time. We found that if we even went a few days without connecting our hearts, we would quickly become agitated with one another, more confrontational, less empathetic, and begin to feel unloved. Daily time to connect became our key to sustaining love and essential to staying in love. We know how busy family can be, but in the bustle of everyday life, taking just fifteen minutes each day to be totally present to one another — to truly listen to what is going on in your spouse's heart, to give and receive love — can strengthen your love and transform your marriage. So, we have sat in our backyard, gone on a walk, locked ourselves in a room, and even sat in a car. We do whatever we reasonably can to have just a little time alone. Next to our time with God, our time with each other is the most important thing on our "to do" list each day.

**Prayer:** Lord, may we make time together a top priority each day so our marriage can thrive according to your holy will for our lives. Amen.

# Day 25

*It is a requisite for the relaxation of the mind that we make use, from time to time, of playful deeds and jokes.*

*— St. Thomas Aquinas*

What separates a happy marriage from a miserable one is how often a couple truly experiences tangible joy within their vocation. The more joy there is, the more manageable life is, the less stress we feel when problems arise, and the stronger our marriage becomes. Kathleen tends to be more serious, so she needs to remind herself to loosen up and let her hair down more often. Troy is more lighthearted; the spirit of playfulness that he brings to our marriage is a blessing. To experience joy, couples need to regularly carve time out to have fun, to laugh, and to enjoy life together. Not every moment of every day needs to be dedicated to serious matters or pursuits. What do you and your spouse enjoy doing together? How do you have fun? Is laughter a frequent guest in your home? It is important to routinely make time and space to enjoy each other's company. And it doesn't have to cost a thing!

**Prayer:** Lord, may there always be a spirit of joy within the walls of our home. Amen.

# DAY 26

*Commit your way to the Lord; trust in him, and he will act.*

*— Psalm 37:5*

Whthen Ginny and Joe were first dating, Ginny did not think much of where their relationship was headed. While Ginny liked Joe and enjoyed his company, she was not ready for a serious, lifelong commitment, so she decided to break things off.

One evening at dinner, prepared to break up with Joe, Ginny heard a voice clearly say, "You will regret it for the rest of your life if you break up with him." Ginny was stunned, but she trusted that God was leading her. Over the next few months she took a deeper look at Joe. She saw his values, his faith, and the way he lived his life with integrity.

Twenty-nine years and three grown children later, Ginny fondly remembers how God led her to her beloved. During challenging times, she goes back to that defining moment in their relationship, because it reminds her of who Joe is at the core and helps her love him despite what she may feel in the moment.

**Prayer:** Lord, may we always be mindful of what first drew our hearts together and trust in your plan for our marriage. Amen.

# DAY 27

*I sought the Lord, and he answered me,*
*and delivered me from all my fears.*

*— Psalm 34:4*

Jeanette was an overwhelmed young mom swallowed by a feeling of having to do it all alone, while Steve felt his wife simply didn't care about him. Both were struggling to communicate well, and feelings of resentment had begun to settle in. It seemed like there was nothing they could say or do to remedy their situation.

One night it occurred to Jeanette that she should pray to the Holy Spirit and ask him for help. She invited Steve to pray with her, and he willingly agreed. They both knew they needed something more than either of them had to give. After uniting their hands and hearts in an urgent plea for help, Jeanette was immediately inspired with more love for her husband, but also received wisdom to know how to show that love to him. From that moment on, everything got better. This experience saved their marriage and taught them both how much they needed God and how powerful it is to call upon the Holy Spirit for help.

**Prayer:** Lord, help us seek you every day and remember to call upon your Holy Spirit to breathe life into our marriage. Amen.

# DAY 28

*The Lord is near to the brokenhearted,*
*and saves the crushed in spirit.*

— *Psalm 34:18*

A few summers ago, Troy was traveling every week to Costa Rica for business. The constant physical distance left little time to reconnect between trips. Eventually, it took a toll on our marriage. One evening between trips, we sat quietly at our favorite restaurant. The air was so thick between us, you could cut it with a knife. After a long spell of silence, Troy said something that slashed Kathleen to the core. She was about to strike back but recalled words a close friend had recently shared with her: "Push into the pain." So she said a prayer to the Holy Spirit and opened her heart wide to receive Troy's words. Ironically, instead of feeling more heartbroken, Kathleen felt even more love for Troy. It was a beautiful beginning toward much-needed healing.

No matter how much we love our spouse, sometimes we will hurt each other. Instead of pulling back for fear of further injury, God calls us to enter into the pain and push through it to an even deeper love.

**Prayer:** Lord, when we are tempted to retreat from one another, may we press in closer through the grace of our sacrament. Amen.

# DAY 29

*The sinner who is sorry for his sins, is closer to God*
*than the just man who boasts of his good works.*

— *St. Pio of Pietrelcina*

Pride draws us into making comparisons. The only person we should compare ourselves to is the one God created us to be. In this way we are always striving to better ourselves instead of becoming arrogant. The same principle holds true for marriage. We might think our marriage is better than Tom and Stacy's marriage, and maybe it truly is. But how will we ever grow together as a couple if we compare our marriage to those that appear to be struggling more than we are? It's helpful to know that there will always be better marriages than ours, and marriages which ours far exceed. Do not be blinded by the sin of pride, but rather live your marriage with Christlike humility. We shouldn't boast about what we do well as a couple. Instead, we need to focus on what needs God's grace. The key to cultivating an exceptional marriage is knowing how to maximize our strengths and learn from our weaknesses. We do well to look to those marriages that we admire and emulate them.

**Prayer:** Lord, help us to be grateful for the strengths of our marriage and be truly sorry for our failings. Amen.

# DAY 30

*Have no anxiety about anything, but in everything*
*by prayer and supplication with thanksgiving*
*let your requests be made known to God.*

*— Philippians 4:6*

God knows we have many concerns on our hearts, and he yearns for us to go to him like little children. Lay each request you have — material, spiritual, emotional, or physical — before the throne of God in hopeful expectation. It may not be how or when you would like, or how you expect, but God will provide, and in a way most suitable for your salvation. If the car breaks down and you do not have the funds to repair it, and yet a working vehicle is essential to providing for your family, ask God specifically for the means to repair or replace the car. If you get laid off from work, ask God to show you where he wants you next and provide the means to pay your bills and care for your family until you secure employment. Our Lord desires for us to be specific in our prayers of petition and then trust him to provide for us and our family.

**Prayer:** Lord, we come to you with expectant hearts and ask that you provide for our needs. Thank you for your provision in our lives. Amen.

# DAY 31

*If God sends you many sufferings it is a sign that He has
great plans for you and certainly wants to make you a saint.*

— *St. Ignatius of Loyola*

With the opportunity to view others' lives through social media, it can be tempting to compare our suffering with that of others. And yet Our Lord asks us to carry our crosses, not compare them. Each cross we are asked to carry builds our spiritual stamina in a way that is specifically and uniquely designed for us. Our greatest suffering is often the launching pad for our greatest mission. Married couples have a responsibility to help each other face the trials of each day and bear one another's burdens. Through the grace of our sacrament in action, the weight is shared, and the crosses are bearable. Can our spouse rely on us in tough times to support them with sacrificial love and help them carry their cross? One of the greatest gifts we can give our spouse is the assurance of our commitment to pass through the storms of life together — hand in hand, hearts united.

**Prayer:** Lord, may we bear one another's burdens in love and trust that you will use them to help us become saints. Amen.

# DAY 32

*For a vacation to be truly such and bring genuine well-being, in it a person must recover a good balance with himself, with others and with the environment. It is this interior and exterior harmony which revitalizes the mind and reinvigorates body and spirit.*

— *Pope St. John Paul II*

Spending quality time together is vital to creating and maintaining a healthy and happy home. Even when resources (time and money) are limited, it's important to take a vacation together now and then. It does not have to be fancy or far away or expensive. The important thing is to simply enjoy life together away from daily responsibilities and pressures. Many families find camping a fun and economical way to vacation. Others like history and visiting historical sites. All it takes is a little research to find the ideal vacation, and part of the bonding is in the planning. Our family enjoys taking road trips, and we have been on many adventures together. These family vacations and couple getaways have fortified our bonds and created some of our most lasting memories. Vacations bring balance, relieve stress, and build the shared experiences we draw on when getting away isn't possible.

**Prayer:** Lord, help us prioritize the value of spending quality time together and please provide the means for us to do so. Amen.

# Day 33

*I cannot believe that a soul which has arrived so
near to Mercy itself, where she knows what she is,
and how many sins God has forgiven her, should
not instantly and willingly forgive others.*

— *St. Teresa of Ávila*

As much as we may want to manipulate or change our spouse's behaviors, it is not our place or responsibility to do so. God reserves the right to change our spouse. What is our duty, though, is to practice mercy through forgiveness. When we acknowledge that we ourselves are sinners, our marriage moves forward in God's grace instead of being stuck in a vicious cycle of tit for tat. In a strong marriage, both husband and wife develop the habit of forgiveness. Each is faithful to forgive and to ask for forgiveness. The words, "I am sorry," sincerely spoken, are some of the most powerful words we can ever utter in marriage. Remember that our spouse is human and will hurt us from time to time, just as we will hurt them. It is these very moments though, when the broken pieces of our marriage are reconciled in love, that create a masterpiece of God's mercy in action.

**Prayer:** Lord, help us be quick to forgive and to ask for forgiveness. May we always exercise mercy in our marriage. Amen.

# DAY 34

*When we leave Mass, we ought to go out the way Moses*
*descended Mt. Sinai: with his face shining, with his*
*heart brave and strong to face the world's difficulties.*

— *St. Oscar Romero*

The Eucharist is the summit of our Faith, and Mass is the highest form of prayer. It is our strength for the journey and our spiritual nourishment to be the best spouse we can be. Because it is the sacrifice of God for us, the Holy Eucharist is the ultimate form of sacrifice and the best example of how we are called to live a sacrificial life of love through the Sacrament of Matrimony. Sunday Mass is essential and required for Catholics, but attending Mass even one additional day during the week can do wonders for your marriage. Is there a way that you can attend Mass more often than just on Sundays? When we receive Jesus in the Eucharist in a state of grace, we are empowered to live our vocation of marriage in a state of grace.

**Prayer**: Lord, thank you for the gift of the Mass and the opportunity to receive you in the Eucharist. May the graces we receive feed our souls and nourish our marriage. Amen.

# Day 35

*Do not be disheartened. I have seen you struggle.*
*Today's defeat is training for tomorrow's victory.*

— *St. Josemaría Escrivá*

Do you ever feel like for every two steps you take forward in your marriage, you take three giant leaps back? There was a season early on in our marriage when we both felt so defeated. We would make tiny advancements forward only to regress again. It was painful, and many days we both felt like giving up. We had much to learn about long-lasting, enduring love in the years to come, and about what it takes to turn defeat into triumph. Little by little, through our commitment to one another, the strength of our faith, and God's grace through our sacrament, we saw our struggles turn into victories, our sorrows into joys, and the weak links in our marriage into strengths. It took time, dedication, persistence, and a lot of prayer to bring us to a solid place in our marriage. Now we can build with more fervor and love the life we know God is asking us to live. Every obstacle we encounter in marriage is an opportunity to grow.

**Prayer:** Lord, give us the grace to receive each obstacle we encounter as an opportunity to love one another more deeply. Amen.

# DAY 36

*I am longing to be near you, my dear Louis. I love
you with all my heart, and I feel my affection so
much more when you're not here with me. It would
be impossible for me to live apart from you.*

— *St. Zélie Martin to St. Louis Martin*

These beautiful and heartfelt sentiments are a model for all married couples. Sadly, countless women over the years have shared with Kathleen how they happily anticipate their husbands' departure for a business trip or an expedition with friends. The truth is that we welcome the physical absence of a spouse when our hearts are wounded. We should want to be together! But if our spouse does not feel loved when we are together, why would they miss us when we are apart? Troy frequently travels for work, and Kathleen often finds herself longing to be near him when he is away. On the practical level, she misses his help. But more importantly, she longs for his presence in the home as the head of our family and the keeper of her heart. We should strive to love so deeply and authentically that when we are physically absent, our spiritual and emotional presence is still felt.

**Prayer:** Lord, help us create a bond of mutual love and respect for one another so when we cannot physically be together, our hearts are still deeply connected. Amen.

# Day 37

*Strive for peace with all men, and for the holiness*
*without which no one will see the Lord.*

*— Hebrews 12:14*

We can be busy with many things that do not last — things like money, activities, and achievements. As Christians, however, we are called to make people our priority, especially those closest to us. Children grow up and move on in the blink of an eye. Spouses grow closer or disconnect from one another. It's amazing to think that something so significant as world peace can be disrupted by what goes on in our homes! Hindsight is always 20/20, but foresight is what allows us to build a life that has eternal value. We will never see a U-Haul® trailer attached to a hearse. We cannot take our riches or worldly accomplishments with us when we leave this world, but we can live a rich life and leave a legacy of love if we take time to invest in our marriage and family now.

**Prayer:** Lord, may we never become so busy that we do not have time to invest in our marriage and family. When we need to reorder our priorities, give us the grace to recognize it and take action. Amen.

# Day 38

*For no matter how numerous our activities, our ministries,
however numerous our concerns, our exertions — if
there is no love, everything becomes meaningless.*

— *Pope St. John Paul II*

Sometimes we need to take a step back and examine whether the commitments we have taken on have actually taken over. If we don't have time for our marriage or family to connect and just be together because we are running from activity to activity, something needs to change. We are tugged at from every direction to give more, be more, and do more, and there are a lot of good things to invest our time in. But when we do not take time for what matters most, what matters most suffers. We do not always have to step in and save the day. If we become someone else's champion but lose the respect of our own spouse and family members, it is crucial that we reexamine our priorities and commitments and make the necessary adjustments to reinvest ourselves in our marriage and family. Love is what gives meaning to everything, and love begins at home.

**Prayer:** Lord, help us to not become so busy doing, that we have no time to invest in loving. Amen.

# DAY 39

*Our words are a faithful index to the state of our souls.*

— *St. Francis de Sales*

What we say — and how we say it — typically reflects what's going on inside of us. Listen carefully to your spouse so you can more fully grasp what's going on in their heart. Likewise, pay close attention to your own words to better understand what may be lurking beneath the surface. Once words leave our mouth, they cannot be retrieved. Instead of blurting out what we think or feel in the moment, Kathleen has learned that she occasionally needs to think calmly and prayerfully through what she genuinely wants to communicate to Troy. When the emotions are high and the pain is raw, consider taking a timeout before saying something you will later regret. And if you do say something hurtful, apologize.

**Prayer:** Lord, help us walk in close union with you so our words reflect a soul in a state of grace. Amen.

# DAY 40

*Above all hold unfailing your love for one another,*
*since love covers a multitude of sins.*

— *1 Peter 4:8*

We are all sinners, and the people with whom we spend the greatest amount of time are the people we are most likely to sin against. It is easier to sin where we expect to be forgiven and loved regardless. Consequently, it is common for us to let loose a little too much and treat our spouse worse than we would treat anyone else. True love expresses compassion and considers the source of the sin. Was she just worn out and tired? Was he overwhelmed from a long day at work? When we love someone, we know that our love is imperfect. We realize that we don't always act in ways that are consistent with the love we are called to live in marriage. That kind of humility is attractive! The good news is that the love we share with our spouse has the potential to outweigh the damage of our occasional sinful actions. By grace, that love is growing every day.

**Prayer:** Lord, whether intentionally or not, we will inevitably sin against one another. When we do, please give us the gift of compassionate hearts and allow our love to cover one another's sins. Amen.

# Day 41

*Bear one another's burdens, and so fulfill the law of Christ.*

— *Galatians 6:2*

After Jesus fell for a third time in utter exhaustion from the weight of the cross on the road to Calvary, a man named Simon of Cyrene was pulled from the crowd to help him. In marriage we are given the special role of being Simon of Cyrene to our spouse. We help carry the cross when our spouse is struggling with the weight and pressure of a particular suffering. Whether our spouse is down and out over a small burden or crushed under the weight of a large cross, we are given the opportunity in these circumstances to showcase our love in a unique and life-giving way. Everyone has a different capacity for pain. It is not up to us to judge the weight of the cross our spouse is carrying, but rather to help them carry it in love.

**Prayer:** Lord, mold my heart to serve you through service to my spouse. When one of us is suffering, strengthen the other, so that we truly bear one another's burdens. Amen.

# DAY 42

*Only the chaste man and the chaste*
*woman are capable of real love.*

— *Pope St. John Paul II*

Chastity does not stop when marriage begins; it simply takes on a more mature meaning. Living chastely within marriage means avoiding anything that violates the dignity of our spouse. That includes committing adultery with another person, using pornography, or engaging in impure actions together. We cannot clearly see our spouse and fully love them for who they are if our vision is skewed by a selfish desire for pleasure. What kind of entertainment do we watch? What do we fill our minds with? Do we use pornography? All these things can hinder our hearts from fully loving our spouse. If your marriage suffers from lack of chastity in some way, do not lose hope. Be honest about your struggle, educate yourself about God's vision for sexuality within marriage, pray for the grace to embrace chastity, and seek help.

**Prayer:** Lord, purify our hearts so we can live our marriage according to your plan for human love. Amen.

# DAY 43

*I have been all things unholy. If God can work
through me, He can work through anyone.*

— *Attrtibuted to St. Francis of Assisi*

At one point or another, we may have felt that we have been less than holy in our marriage. The good news is that God can and will use us despite our failings and sins. For that to occur, we need to do what we can to keep ourselves in a state of grace. A successful marriage requires that we tap into the graces available through all the sacraments. We cannot live our marriages in union with God and be truly happy if we are in serious sin. Even venial sins present obstacles to grace that can grow over time. Going to confession restores our relationship with God and removes the obstacles to love in our hearts. Our family tries to make a point of going to confession at least once a month. Now that some of our children are older, they will often go to confession on their own. Find what works for your family and do what it takes to make the Sacrament of Reconciliation a regular habit.

**Prayer:** Lord, help us stay right with you so we can be a vessel of your grace to one another in our marriage. Amen.

# DAY 44

*The lot is cast into the lap, but the*
*decision is wholly from the Lord.*

*— Proverbs 16:33*

God brought you and your spouse together for a specific plan and purpose. It was not chance that you met, but part of God's design for your lives to mold you into the people he desires each of you to become. God will use both good and bad times as part of the path he set your feet on together as a married couple; do not be fearful of embracing both. Trust that each moment, each situation contributes to the bigger picture of God's purpose and plan for your life together. If you desire to experience true happiness and fulfillment in your vocation, seek God's will for your marriage. Ask God to show you why he brought you together. It may not be clear all at once, but God will reveal his blueprint to you little by little as his plan for your life together unfolds.

**Prayer:** Lord, we know you have a specific plan and purpose for our life together. Help us to seek your will each day and follow the path you lay before us. Amen.

# Day 45

*Pray, hope and don't worry. Worry is useless.*
*God is merciful and will hear your prayer.*

— *St. Pio of Pietrelcina*

Until a recent kitchen remodel, we had this quote hanging above our kitchen sink as a reminder to trust God in all circumstances. Kathleen often thinks of herself as the "Project Manager" of our home. There are always numerous tasks to accomplish, and these words are a good reminder that while worry is truly useless, prayer is always worthwhile. When our minds begin to fill with worry over the situations we find ourselves in each day, we can reach out to God in prayer. We tell him our concerns and ask him to show us how to best handle our current state of affairs. Let God carry the weight of our burdens, trust in his power and love, and have hope in knowing that God makes all things beautiful in his time.

**Prayer:** Lord, when we begin to sink under the pressures of life, help us set worries aside and trust in you. Amen.

# DAY 46

*For here we have no lasting city, but we*
*seek the city which is to come.*

— *Hebrews 13:14*

We are all on a journey to heaven, our ultimate home and final destination. Our vocation in life is our "ship" that takes us there. When we were first married, Kathleen naively thought that "holy actions" and living a virtuous life was her role in advancing Troy on his way to heaven. Eventually, she realized that having to deal with her own sinfulness has assisted him more. We are challenged to grow in love and virtue every time our spouse fails to act the way they should.

Place God at the helm of your marriage. Be mindful of where your ship is headed; don't let the storms distract you. And don't forget your need for God when waters are calm. Praise him in the calm and in the storm. Keep your eyes fixed on his compass for your marriage and sail in the direction he leads you. Don't jump ship, lest you drown; instead hang on and enjoy the voyage!

**Prayer:** Lord, when we are tempted to jump ship out of pain or fear, help us to cling to you and recognize we are in this ship together to get one another to heaven. Amen.

# Day 47

*I am not capable of doing big things, but*
*I want to do everything, even the smallest*
*things, for the greater glory of God.*

— *St. Dominic Savio*

We are called to holiness within our homes. It is here, in the trenches of day-to-day life, that our actions and words have the most meaning. It is natural to want to be recognized for good behavior and virtuous acts, but our spouse might not always give us the affirmation we desire. Often, that is because we are seeking virtue in bigger things instead of remaining content with the small, everyday acts that are always available to us. Our spouse ought to receive the best of us, but what frequently happens is we give our spouse the scraps left over at the end of the day.

Begin your day together with a loving embrace and kiss; check in with each other as possible throughout the day — a phone call, a text — then make time for one another when you reunite in the evening. Remember that the smallest things can bring glory to God.

**Prayer:** Lord, help us to see you in the smallest things and always be mindful that as we serve and love each other, we are serving and loving you. Amen.

# DAY 48

*Anything that does not lead you to God is a*
*hindrance. Root it out and throw it far from you.*

— *St. Josemaría Escrivá*

Life is going to throw us enough obstacles to overcome; it's wise not to contribute more by welcoming people and circumstances into our life and marriage that take us away from God. Anything that does not lead us to God is a hindrance to happiness. Life is a gift and is meant to be fully lived and enjoyed. We should have fun, take trips, dance, laugh, recreate, build, create — we just want to be sure God is directing us. If things or people are currently hindering us from living in God's grace or from tapping into the sacramental grace of our marriage, we should root them out as swiftly as possible. When we rid ourselves of that which is drawing us away, we will experience more peace and joy in marriage than we ever thought possible.

**Prayer:** Lord, help us to identify everything in our lives that does not lead us closer to you. Give us the courage to remove these things and discover the true happiness you desire for us. Amen.

# Day 49

*[Love] is … not resentful.*

— *1 Corinthians 13:5*

There is no place for resentment in marriage. Resentment only leads to bitterness, and bitterness is inconsistent with love. We cannot love and resent someone simultaneously. Whenever we are wronged, we are called to prompt forgiveness, even if the person who hurt us does not apologize — and even if the person who hurt us is our husband or wife. It may not be easy to forgive. It may not even seem fair. But holding onto grudges can never strengthen a relationship, and resentment poisons a marriage the way few things can. Part of how we are called to die to self and selfishness is letting go of scorekeeping. Holding onto each other is much more difficult when we are holding something against each other.

**Prayer:** Lord, help us let go of any resentments we may have with one another so we can live in the freedom of your love. Amen.

# DAY 50

*Know that even when you are in the kitchen, Our*
*Lord is moving among the pots and pans.*

— *St. Teresa of Ávila*

This quote hangs on a crafted piece of wood in our kitchen as a reminder that God is present in the mundane tasks of everyday life. When Kathleen is tired and worn out from preparing the third meal of the day (not including snacks!), and washing what feels like the hundredth plate, she looks at these words and is reminded of *why*. Why do we do what we do for our family, for our husband or wife? We do it because we love them and long for heaven. We believe that fully embracing our vocation is our means to get there. God is present and active in each task we do, big and small. He moves among the pots and pans. He wants to transform the ordinary moments of our lives into extraordinary moments of love.

**Prayer:** Lord, open our eyes to see you working in each moment of our lives and in particular our marriage. Amen.

# Day 51

*Every home should be a haven of peace and serenity in
spite of the small frustrations of daily life. An atmosphere
of profound and sincere affection should reign there
together with a deep-rooted calm, which is the result
of an authentic faith that is put into practice.*

— *St. Josemaría Escrivá*

What is the atmosphere of your home? Is it a safe and calm shelter, or more like a battleground? It's easy to fall into a negative pattern and allow a negative atmosphere to grow. That's why it is good to evaluate the overall ambiance of our home from time to time. To paraphrase Saint Josemaría, a peaceful home is the result of a lived, authentic faith. Sometimes longstanding hurts make it hard to cultivate a peaceful atmosphere. Don't try to fix them on your own power. Put them all — and each other — into God's hands in prayer. Stay close to God, keep your faith real, invest in your marriage, and the eventual result will be a home that you both will want to come home to.

**Prayer:** Lord, make our home a peaceful haven where you permanently reside in communion with our family. Amen.

# DAY 52

*Love is patient and kind; love is not jealous or boastful.*

*— 1 Corinthians 13:4*

Saint Paul helps us consider what love is, and what it isn't. In marriage we are given ample opportunities to practice patience, from annoying habits and behaviors, to marital misunderstandings, to our need for help in difficult situations. When we are patient with our spouse, we express our authentic love for them. There are times when we don't feel like being kind to each other. Still, we know that love calls us to show genuine kindness regardless of how we feel and despite how much we might inwardly struggle in the moment. Remember that two become one in marriage, so it does us no good to be jealous. Rather, we should delight in our spouse's opportunities, advancements, and achievements. After all, we are on the same side headed toward the same ultimate goal. Finally, humility is attractive, and arrogance is appalling. When we witness the other practicing sincere humility, we fall deeper in love. A solid marriage is built on genuine love. Align yourself with what love really is and watch your marriage blossom.

**Prayer:** Lord, help us live the virtues of patience and kindness in our marriage, and keep envy and boastfulness far from us. Amen.

# Day 53

*[Love] is not arrogant or rude.*
*Love does not insist on its own way.*

— *1 Corinthians 13:5*

We sin most against those we love most. The deeper our love for someone, the more pain we experience when we are wronged by them, and the more tempted we are to retaliate or shut down. But feeling hurt can lead us to selfishness and self-protection. Insisting on our way may initially calm our heart and make us feel better, but it never succeeds. It only causes more pain and builds a wall between us and our spouse. Only selflessness breaks the wall down and opens our spouse's heart to receive our love. Troy has often expressed love through his selfless acts of service, even when Kathleen didn't deserve it. What is most beautiful though, is that good begets good; an act of service inspires selflessness. When we both die to ourselves, our marriage is fully alive!

**Prayer:** Lord, help us die to our selfishness so our marriage can fully live in you! Amen.

# DAY 54

*[Love] it is not irritable.*

*— 1 Corinthians 13:5*

We recognize that when we don't take care of ourselves physically, spiritually, and mentally — and especially when we don't get enough sleep — we are prone to irritability. Being on edge and irritable with our spouse creates a tense environment and can make us feel like we have to walk on eggshells.

Do what you need to do to prevent being short-tempered with your spouse. Get plenty of sleep, eat healthy, exercise, and pray — all are ways that help avoid the feeling of irritability. There will be times that medical conditions or a stressful situation might make it difficult to avoid being irritable. When your spouse is struggling, don't be insensitive. Instead, give them the support they need by being patient and understanding and love them through it.

**Prayer:** Lord, help us take care of ourselves physically, spiritually, and mentally so we can be our best selves for our spouse. Amen.

# DAY 55

*[Love] does not rejoice at wrong, but rejoices in the right.*

*— 1 Corinthians 13:6*

The struggle to live a righteous, holy life is real. Do you recognize and encourage your spouse's efforts, big and small, each day to advance in virtue? When Kathleen rejoices in what Troy is doing right, Troy is further motivated to up his game. Her affirmation and encouragement are like fuel to his soul. It helps him to step up to be the spiritual leader of our family as God is calling him to be. Conversely, when Kathleen withholds her appreciation because of pain or fear, Troy feels discouraged and demotivated. Spouses are walking together toward heaven, and the path is narrow. The path to hell, on the other hand, is wide. It is important to be purposeful in our praise of what our spouse is doing right, the good decisions made, and the positive actions lived. This practice furthers us as a couple on the path of holiness and helps us avoid the pitfalls that can cause us to detour in the wrong direction.

**Prayer:** Lord, help us rejoice in one another's efforts to live upright and holy lives so we can support each other on our journey together. Amen.

# Day 56

*No one can be ready for the next life unless he trains himself for it now.*

— *St. Augustine of Hippo*

The older we get, the more we realize how essential it is to stay on top of our health. Kathleen enjoys exercising but consistently healthy eating is a challenge. With Troy's support, Kathleen recently hired a personal trainer to give her the boost she needs to get on the right track. The trainer teaches and guides Kathleen, holds her accountable, and encourages her when she gets discouraged. She can't, however, do Kathleen's work for her. In our spiritual life, the Holy Spirit is our personal trainer. He teaches, guides, holds us accountable, and encourages us on our journey to heaven. Because we have free will, though, God is not going to drag us. We have to choose to be purposeful through each goal we set, each decision we make, each action we take, and each cross we bear. These train us for eternal life with Christ. This life is intended to prepare us for the next, and our vocation of marriage is how we will get there.

**Prayer:** Lord, help us train in this life through the vocation of our marriage so we can spend eternal life with you. Amen.

# Day 57

*I am the Lord;*
*in its time I will hasten it.*

*— Isaiah 60:22*

How often in marriage do we hope and pray for something to change that is causing us heartache? Perhaps our spouse is away from the Faith, our husband has lost his job, our wife has a debilitating illness, or our relationship has been broken by lies and betrayal. In all situations we are called to wait on God and persevere in faith, trusting that in his time our prayers will be answered. Waiting is never easy, especially when the answer may not be what we hope and pray for. We can, however, trust that it is the way God sees is best for our spiritual growth. Everything God allows us to experience in life has a purpose — one that in his time he will reveal. God's timing is perfect, and our task is to grow in trust. When we insist on our way, we push God out of the picture. When we accept his will and his timing, we find ourselves part of a picture more beautiful than we ever imagined.

**Prayer:** Lord, help us trust in your perfect timing in every aspect of our lives. Amen.

# DAY 58

*[Spouses are] the permanent reminder to the*
*Church of what happened on the cross.*

— *Pope St. John Paul II*

Husbands and wives are called in the Sacrament of Matrimony to mirror the sacrificial self-gift of Christ to his Church. Jesus gave himself completely by dying on the cross so the Church could be born and the gates of heaven opened. In marriage we are repeatedly commissioned to die to ourselves for the sake of a greater good — for peace in our marriage, for harmony in our home, for the spiritual growth of our spouse and ourselves, for the holiness of our family. When we take this calling seriously and willingly die to our own selfish wants and ways, beautiful things are born. Jesus asks us to follow his example of selfless love for our bride and for our groom. This is authentic love, and to live it requires that we surrender our will in how we want to live our vocation as a married person and follow God's will instead.

**Prayer:** Lord, help us mirror in our marriage your love for us on the cross. Amen.

# Day 59

*No one heals himself by wounding another.*

— *St. Ambrose of Milan*

Unfortunately, because of the fall of Adam and Eve, it is inevitable that we will inflict wounds upon our spouse. Sadly, we often make the mistake of thinking we can heal ourselves or expect our spouse to heal the wound they created. It is important to validate the hurt we caused our spouse so they feel understood, but we cannot heal the wounds we inflict. Only God can heal our wounds. Most hurts are unintentional, but if we fall into the trap of thinking that retaliation is going to sooth our wounds and make us feel better, we will only create more and deeper wounds. Living marriage in a tit-for-tat cycle gets us nowhere. If you find yourself living your marriage this way, we urge you to jump off the hamster wheel and break free from this spiteful and sinful cycle. Ask God to heal your wounds and offer your spouse the forgiveness they need.

**Prayer:** Lord, heal us and free us from the wounds we have caused one another. Amen.

# Day 60

*It is better to limp along the right path than to
walk strongly in the wrong direction.*

— *St. Augustine of Hippo*

Many of the decisions that will have the most impact on our marriage will not be between what is right and wrong, but between what is good and what is better. There will constantly be good things to do, but it is important to make decisions based on what's right for our marriage and family. Is it OK to go out with friends one night a week? Perhaps, but does that mean we are sacrificing the only night to spend time with our spouse? Is it OK to watch our favorite sports on television a few hours a week? Maybe, but in doing so are we neglecting our responsibilities around the house? Only we can answer these questions. The key is to find balance and make sure that good things do not take away from the best thing, and that decisions are made together as a couple mindful of the final destination: heaven.

**Prayer:** Lord, help us daily discern between what is good and what is your will. Provide us with the fortitude to persevere — even slowly — on the right path. Amen.

# Day 61

*Who except God can give you peace? Has the
world ever been able to satisfy the heart?*

— *St. Gerard Majella*

We want peace in our marriage and in our home. Daily stresses can overwhelm us, and we just want a haven to come home to. There are a lot of moving parts in a family, however, and creating an atmosphere of peace amid a lot of activity can be challenging. So how do we find peace in the often-chaotic flurry of daily life? The truth is that our spouse cannot give us peace, our work will not provide it, and our children will certainly challenge it. Nothing this world has to offer will satiate our longing. The only way to find true peace is through a personal relationship with God. That's why we begin our day with prayer, check in with God throughout the day, seek his will in all we do, pray as a couple and with our family, and pray before we go to bed. If we stay connected to God, the atmosphere of our marriage and our home will begin to change as we experience true peace.

**Prayer:** Lord, please help us stay close to you as a couple and as a family so we may be filled with your peace. Amen.

# DAY 62

*Every branch of mine that bears no fruit, he*
*takes away, and every branch that does bear fruit*
*he prunes, that it may bear more fruit.*

*— John 15:2*

In the dead of winter, Troy prunes the vines in our small family vineyard. As he chops, cuts, and makes a gnarled mess of grapes vines, he removes diseased branches that could infect the entire vine, but also perfectly healthy branches. Why? Too many branches growing on the vine prevent optimal sunlight from reaching the budding grapes, thereby yielding a smaller harvest. Too many branches keep the vine from harnessing its energy for making grapes. Instead, its energy is divided among all the healthy branches just to keep them alive.

We all have both healthy and unhealthy branches that need pruning in order for our souls to produce abundant fruit. What diseased branches need to be cut off in our life? In our marriage? What addictions or disordered attachments? What about those healthy branches? Are there things taking away from the energy we could otherwise put into developing the beauty of our interior life and relationship with our spouse? What healthy branches need pruning in our life or in our marriage?

**Prayer:** Lord, give us the wisdom to know what needs pruning in our lives in order to have a healthier and more fruitful marriage. Amen.

# DAY 63

*Do not, therefore, abandon that confidence*
*of yours; it brings a great reward.*

— *Hebrews 10:35 (NRSV-CE)*

Just because something is in your head doesn't automatically mean that it is actually true. Remember not to abandon your confidence. It can be tempting for us to conjure up stories in our heads before we have all the facts. When we do, we are trading the confidence and trust we have in one another for suspicion and doubt. When husbands and wives feel secure in their love for one another, the temptation to think negatively is less prominent — even nonexistent — when, for whatever reason, facts are missing or communication is lacking. We should trust in our spouse's good nature and love for us until all the facts have been made known and the truth is fully revealed. Our confidence in each other will bring us great reward.

**Prayer:** Lord, help us feel confident in our love for one another. Amen.

# Day 64

*Therefore, since we are surrounded by so great a*
*cloud of witnesses, let us also lay aside every weight,*
*and sin which clings so closely, and let us run with*
*perseverance the race that is set before us.*

— *Hebrews 12:1*

We approached some dear friends after Mass to say hello. That's when Michael and Denise told us that he had just been diagnosed with Stage IV colorectal cancer. Our hearts sank. Denise and Michael were both avid runners, but on that day, they embarked on a whole new kind of race. Despite many setbacks and agonizing moments, the strong faith and tenacity this couple displayed was inspiring, and the evident love between them was powerful and attractive. The support and prayers of the community surrounded them and upheld them through the most difficult marathon of their lives.

All couples will be presented with challenging races to run throughout their marriage, some more strenuous than others. It's wise to build our stamina now. The deep faith and love both Michael and Denise had before the diagnosis are what empowered them to endure one of the most excruciating seasons of their marriage.

**Prayer:** Lord, help us develop spiritual stamina and a deep love for one another so we may faithfully run each race you set before us. Amen.

# Day 65

*But all things should be done decently and in order.*

*— 1 Corinthians 14:40*

When things are not appropriately ordered in our marriage and family life, our home will be disordered. God must come first for us, marriage second, children third, and then our job. Our spouse may not demand our time, but our jobs and our children most certainly will. Therefore, we must be purposeful in safeguarding our relationship with our spouse — after our relationship with God. If we allow ourselves to give into the things that compete for our time and allow our priorities to become disordered, confusion and chaos will ensue. But if we keep order in our priorities, our lives will follow.

**Prayer:** Lord, help us develop proper priorities and maintain well-ordered lives so we can know peace in our marriage and family life. Amen.

# DAY 66

*If I did not simply live from one moment to another,*
*it would be impossible for me to be patient, but*
*I only look at the present. I forget the past, and*
*I take good care not to forestall the future.*

— *St. Thérèse of Lisieux*

Do we let past hurts dictate our current actions? Hanging onto a grudge merely weighs us down and disables us from wholly loving in the present moment. God desires for us to move forward from injury and unforgiveness in light of the past, not be crippled by it. We will inevitably hurt one another. It is what we do with the hurt that determines the amount of pain it will ultimately cause us individually and together as a couple. Learn from the past and let go of it. Live one moment at a time and embrace each moment as it comes. We should cautiously navigate our past wounds — including those we suffered before we even met our spouse — and be careful not to allow them to jeopardize the current health of our marriage.

**Prayer:** Lord, give us the grace needed to love in each moment as you would have us love. Help us let go of past wounds so we may be free to cultivate our marriage according to your will. Amen.

# DAY 67

*Put love where there is no love, and you will draw out love.*

*— St. John of the Cross*

Is your marriage running on fumes, or worse yet — is your love tank completely empty? Perhaps you no longer feel "in love" with your spouse, or maybe you no longer love them at all. What would you do differently if you were "in love" with your spouse, if you *did* feel love for them?

We've learned that when we do those things, even when we don't feel like loving each other, things change. Do the things you would do as if you were "in love," as if you simply loved your spouse; show them respect, spend time with them, smile at them, embrace them, listen to them. If you do, you will see a transformation gradually take place. For when we put love where there is no love, love will grow.

**Prayer:** Lord, help us to love one another consistently and wholly despite how we may feel in a particular moment or season of our marriage. Amen.

# Day 68

*Christ beside me, Christ before me, Christ behind me,*
*Christ within me, Christ beneath me, Christ above me.*

— *St. Patrick*

Saint Patrick got it. He knew that if he was to become a saint, Christ had to be a part of every aspect of his life. This is what we are called to as husbands and wives: to summon Christ into every dimension of our lives, every facet of our marriage vocation. Have we hidden certain sins in a dark closet? Whatever we are keeping tucked away must be exposed to the light. Will it be painful? Probably. But just as a physical wound can only completely heal once it has been exposed to air and light, our sinful selves need to be exposed to forgiveness and love. Sin festers and creates more baggage in darkness, but once it is exposed to light, its oxygen supply is cut off and it dies. Then healing can begin. We invite Christ into every area of our life and marriage so we don't miss out on everything beautiful that God longs to do in and through us, individually and as a married couple.

**Prayer:** Lord, we invite you to be fully present in every aspect of our marriage and we ask that you help us be forthright in all our actions. Amen.

# DAY 69

*He who loves pleasure will be a poor man;*
*he who loves wine and oil will not be rich.*

*— Proverbs 21:17*

Lent is a time to check our Catholic compass, a time set aside to take an honest look at what direction we are moving. But any time of year can be used as a time for reflection on where we've been and what's ahead. It helps to contemplate what we have done in the past year to stretch beyond our comfort zone in seeking God's will and reflect on the fears, struggles, and insecurities that have held us back from fully embracing it. Pleasure is not the purpose of life. Yet we all spend a lot of time and energy trying to attain as much pleasure as we can. Is there a cross we have been asked to carry recently? Is our marriage in the desert? Fully embracing our cross is an opportunity for deep spiritual growth and an opportunity for our marriage to grow and mature. Often our greatest path to holiness is simply embracing the crosses we are given to carry, especially within the vocation of our marriage.

**Prayer:** Lord, may we take the opportunity to check our compass and deepen our relationship with you and with one another. Amen.

# Day 70

*If a man finds it very hard to forgive injuries, let him
look at a crucifix, and think that Christ shed all his
blood for him, and not only forgave his enemies, but
even prayed his heavenly Father to forgive them also.*

— *St. Philip Neri*

At our former parish, we were the co-directors of a marriage ministry called Building Amazing Marriages. Once a month we offered a marriage enrichment date night, which consisted of a short presentation, couple discussion, dinner, and prayer. One of our most well attended date nights each year was our Couple's Stations of the Cross during Lent. Each participant was asked to write down something they planned to sacrifice that Lent for their spouse and their marriage. After praying the Stations, each couple would bring their written sacrifices outside to a bonfire. The feedback we received year after year was that after praying the Stations of the Cross as a couple, husbands and wives were more aware not only of the need to sacrifice for their spouse, but also of how much their spouse sacrificed for them.

**Prayer:** Lord, may we never lose sight of the sacrifice you made out of love for each one of us. Help us to be aware of the loving sacrifices each one of us makes for the other. Amen.

# Day 71

*We are an Easter people and alleluia is our song!*

— *Pope St. John Paul II*

When Kathleen was growing up, her mom often reminded her and her siblings that every Good Friday is followed by an Easter Sunday. We will experience Good Fridays in marriage, but we should never lose hope. Our song is not one of despair, but of victory, even in the face of difficulty! Body builders challenge themselves each week with more weight because they know that this builds their muscles stronger and creates greater endurance. Muscles further develop the more stress they endure; they actually tear and then rebuild more robust than before. Similarly, in the spiritual life, God occasionally allows us to break and tear under the weight of the crosses he asks us to carry, so he can make our faith stronger. We can trust that each difficult moment we walk through, each cross we bear, will be followed by an Easter Sunday. God always brings beauty from the challenging and painful moments of our lives. He uses all things, all situations, for our salvation and greater good.

**Prayer:** Lord, help us embrace the crosses you send us so we can develop our spiritual muscles and deepen our spiritual lives. Amen.

# DAY 72

*The saints were able to make the great journey of
human existence in the way that Christ had done before
them, because they were brimming with great hope.*

— *Pope Benedict XVI*

The two of us recently took a trip to Palm Springs, California. When we left Chicago, it was cloudy and dreary, however, within minutes of taking off, the plane rose above the clouds where the sun was shining brightly. Often in life we have to make a conscious decision to rise above a situation. Despite our circumstances, we can choose to be the better person, let a hurt roll off our shoulders, shine light in the darkness, find beauty in the ashes, be the voice of faith or reason, and love when it is difficult. When we rise above a challenging situation, we are choosing hope. We will always have control over our own actions, but we may not have control over a situation. We may be rightly angry about the way things are, but with courage, we can change them by rising above the clouds.

**Prayer:** Lord, give us hope and strength to rise above the difficult situations in life and courage to act in faith when we are called to make a difference. Amen.

# DAY 73

*And it is my prayer that your love may abound more*
*and more, with knowledge and all discernment.*

*— Philippians 1:9*

Kathleen has enjoyed gardening since childhood. She has also come to appreciate the many life lessons learned and reinforced through the art of gardening. For plants to grow they need basic care: well-prepared soil to grow in, water, and sun. In order for plants to thrive, though, extra measures need to be taken. Weeds must be promptly uprooted before their roots grow too deep. Plants should be protected from predators to avoid damage. And finally, for a plant to grow to its fullest potential, it should be periodically fertilized. The same basic care should be provided in marriage if we want love to grow. However, if we want our marriage to not just grow but thrive, we must be intentional. This means uprooting everyone and everything that threatens the health of our marriage, putting hedges around our marriage to protect it from damage, and fertilizing our marriage by going the extra mile in sacrificial self-gift.

**Prayer:** Lord, help us discern how to best guard, protect, and nourish our marriage so our love for one another can grow and flourish to full potential. Amen.

# DAY 74

*Be who you are meant to be, and you will set the world on fire.*

— *St. Catherine of Siena*

One spring, we crossed an item off our bucket list and visited the Grand Canyon for the first time! What is it that makes the Grand Canyon so attractive and inspiring? For Kathleen, it's the sheer depth of it — the layers upon layers of sediment that the canyon reveals, each representing a specific point in time, each adding its own color and unique beauty to the whole. As we witnessed the view along the South Rim, we reflected on how the Canyon is an image of our interior life. The more layers are revealed, the more beautiful we become. The more depth there is to us, the more striking we are. Forming depth takes time, perseverance, and courage. Just like the attractive layers of sediment in the Grand Canyon were created and then revealed over time, so, too, our interior life grows and develops. Each moment in prayer, each sacrifice made, each temptation resisted, each act of love: these form the layers of our interior life and create depth to our soul.

**Prayer:** Lord, deepen us through the vocation of our marriage. Help us to be who you created us to be, both individually and as a couple. Amen.

# Day 75

*O God, you have made us for yourself, and our*
*hearts are restless until they rest in you.*

— *St. Augustine of Hippo*

Marriage is a wonderful thing, but it is important to remember that our spouse will never fully satisfy us. They are not meant to. We are made by God and for him. He never intended for us to place the burden of this expectation on our spouse. And yet, it can be tempting at times to expect our spouse to fulfill all our needs. When we place unrealistic demands on our husband or wife, it puts a strain on our marriage. This is a burden and weight none of us were ever meant to carry. No one — not even our spouse — is capable of providing complete fulfillment for another person. God alone can satisfy every longing of our heart.

**Prayer:** Lord, help us place only realistic expectations upon one another and find our ultimate fulfillment in you alone. Amen.

# DAY 76

*I want my brethren and kinsfolk to know my nature so
that they may be able to perceive my soul's desire.*

— *St. Patrick*

We all want to be known and loved for who we are at the deepest level of our being. As husbands and wives, it is our responsibility to know our spouse as thoroughly as we can. Do we know our spouse's nature so we can truly see their soul's desire? Do we take a sincere interest in our spouse's life — what they do throughout the day, who their friends are, what they value, what hurts them or makes them happy? When Troy asks Kathleen questions about her day, she can tell that he really wants to know the answer and not simply appear to take an interest. Kathleen wants Troy to truly know her, and when she senses his genuine interest in her life, she feels motivated to assure Troy of her love for him. Married couples spend their whole lives getting to know each other better and better. The more we know one another, the more deeply we can love one another.

**Prayer:** Lord, may we truly know and love one another as you have always intended for married couples from the beginning. Amen.

# Day 77

*In him we live and move and have our being.*

— *Acts 17:28*

If you have ever flown on an airplane before, you have been through the drill of how to properly put your oxygen mask on in the event of a loss of cabin pressure. If you were traveling with children, it was further communicated to make sure your own mask was secure before putting your child's mask on — because if you are not able to breathe properly, you cannot help your child. We cannot give what we do not already have ourselves.

We attended a memorable wedding Mass several years ago. In his homily, the priest stated that the couple being married that day had fallen in love with God before they fell in love with each other. How beautiful! Whether or not this could be said of us, it is important to allow God to breathe life into our soul and our marriage. We need oxygen to breathe, but we need God to live abundantly!

**Prayer:** Lord, be our oxygen; live in us and breathe life into every dimension of our marriage. Amen.

# DAY 78

*Saint Joseph was a just man, a tireless worker, the
upright guardian of those entrusted to his care. May
he always guard, protect and enlighten families.*

— *Pope St. John Paul II*

Ever wonder why Saint Joseph is the only saint from the Holy Family without any dialogue in the Bible? Perhaps it's because we sometimes need to be reminded that actions speak louder than words. Saint Joseph followed God's will when he agreed to accept the Virgin Mary, impregnated by the Holy Spirit, to be his wife. He followed God's will when he fled with his wife and newborn Child, the savior of the world, to Egypt to avoid slaughter. He labored hard as a carpenter to support his family. He passed along his trade — and his Jewish faith — to Jesus. While assuredly Saint Joseph must have been exhausted at times, he persevered with faith, hope, trust, and confidence. There is no biblical account nor hint of Saint Joseph complaining or claiming to be a victim because he was mistreated. Indeed, he utters not a single word. He accepts his role faithfully — as we all are called to do in fulfilling our vocation as husbands and fathers, wives and mothers.

**Prayer:** Lord, help us to model our lives after the life of the Holy Family. Saint Joseph, pray for us. Amen.

# DAY 79

*I can do all things in him who strengthens me.*

*— Philippians 4:13*

Marriage is hard and requires work on the part of both spouses to be successful. The good news is that by the grace of the Sacrament of Matrimony, we have all we need to build a dynamic, holy, and happy marriage. We have weathered countless storms in our marriage, and in the midst of each storm, we have had to cling to the hope that God will give us the strength to survive it and come out stronger on the other side. The key is to hang in there when the going gets tough. This is our calling in life and our way to holiness!

Be brave and be bold! Know that each tumultuous season that God allows you to walk through, he will also provide the grace necessary for your marriage to become stronger through it. We may not be able to do everything on our own. But there is nothing we cannot do without God's grace.

**Prayer:** Lord, we have faith that we can do all things through you. Help us to rely on your strength in every season of our marriage so we may cultivate a deeper and stronger love. Amen.

# Day 80

*Trust in the Lord with all your heart,*
*and do not rely on your own insight.*
*In all your ways acknowledge him,*
*and he will make straight your paths.*

— *Proverbs 3:5–6*

Sometimes things just don't make sense, from the little everyday annoyances to the larger life-changing events. *Why did this happen? Now I am going to be late for work and today is that important meeting. Why can't I get rid of this cold? I am so tired these days. Why would God allow our child to suffer like this? We are heartbroken. Why do we have to move and leave our home? Why does one of us have to travel so much for work or put in long hours? This is so hard on our family. Why?* We may never have the answer to our questions this side of heaven, but we are asked not to rely on our own understanding. Instead, we are challenged to trust that all things happen for a reason and are part of God's bigger plan for our lives and our marriage. In the moment we might not understand, but when we look back, we can often see why God allowed or didn't allow something.

**Prayer:** Lord, help us trust you in every area of our marriage, even when we don't understand our circumstances or your plan. Amen.

# Day 81

*I press on toward the goal for the prize of the*
*upward call of God in Christ Jesus.*

— *Philippians 3:14*

Whether you have personal goals, business goals, family goals, or marriage goals, tackling a small portion each day adds up significantly over time. Both of us are goal-driven individuals, but sometimes staying the course to achieve our objectives can be daunting. Having a clearly defined goal set through prayer, a conviction that this is what God is calling me to do, and a game plan of how to achieve it — this is what motivates us each day to keep going. Our ultimate goal must be to get to heaven, and we need to be determined to stay on the right path to get there, united with our spouse. A few steps in the wrong direction every day can drastically alter our direction and send us completely off-course — perhaps without even realizing it. So we press on a little bit each day, bear our crosses in light of our salvation, love our family deeply, make decisions prayerfully, and live our vocation of marriage as faithfully as we can.

**Prayer:** Lord, help us to align our worldly goals with our final goal of eternal life with you. Amen.

# Day 82

*Not that I complain of want; for I have learned,*
*in whatever state I am, to be content.*

*— Philippians 4:11*

Contentment is not easy to come by today. We are bombarded from every angle to do more, be more, rush more, and desire more. It can be exhausting! But Christ asks us to find rest in him and to be content with where he has us and with what he has given us. When we strive to keep our priorities in order, we will discover that contentment comes from the correct ordering of our life. When challenging moments arrive on the scene with our spouse, we can be satisfied knowing that God is gracious, and that contentment does not depend on what we have or don't have.

**Prayer:** Lord, help us keep our priorities rightly ordered and be content with the vocation you have called us to in the Sacrament of Matrimony. Amen.

# Day 83

*Judge not, that you be not judged. For with the
judgment you pronounce you will be judged, and the
measure you give will be the measure you get. Why
do you see the speck that is in your brother's eye, but
do not notice the log that is in your own eye?*

*— Matthew 7:1–3*

In the early years of our marriage, Kathleen couldn't comprehend why Troy didn't understand certain things. *Doesn't he know that bothers me? Why would he do that AGAIN? I already told him that hurts.* In pride and naivety, she didn't realize that she was judging and misjudging so much about Troy. She expected him to know her without really getting to know him. A good marriage takes time to cultivate and grow, and if we take out our magnifying glasses and critique every little thing about one another, then we hinder that growth. Instead of pointing out their faults, we need to search our hearts and see where we can grow to be a better spouse for them. We need to sincerely get to know our spouse so we can better love them — not so they can better love us. We do that when we stop judging and focus on loving.

**Prayer:** Lord, we lay down our judgments of one another and ask for the humility to see ourselves and one another clearly so we can strive to love each other well. Amen.

# DAY 84

*My children, should death strike now, would you be ready?*

— *St. John Bosco*

While recently attending a parish mission, Troy noticed an elderly lady on Facetime with an elderly man. Afterward, Troy approached her and inquired who she was sharing the speaker with via Facetime. She told him it was her husband who was in a nursing home at the time. She stated that he would have loved to have been there with her, but since he was not able, she decided to bring the parish mission to him! This is true love — the kind that prepares us for heaven! When we are tempted to not be the best husband or wife, we consider that every act we do or don't do is getting us one step closer to eternal paradise, or one step farther away. Death is inevitable and may come unexpectedly. Yet, every day we are provided opportunities to prepare for it through loving our spouse.

**Prayer:** Lord, train our hearts every day through our acts of love for one another to be prepared for eternal life with you. Amen.

# DAY 85

*Begin again.*

— *St. Teresa of Ávila*

Only two words, but with so much meaning and depth to them that give us hope! Marriage requires great perseverance and commitment. We all mess up from time to time in marriage because we are not perfect. Our spouse isn't perfect either. But all we need to move forward is the willingness to continually "begin again" when we fall. Every day is, and can be, a new beginning. It doesn't matter how many times we start over, just that we do. God is there to give us the grace of a fresh start. We can learn to be there for one another to make beginning again a way of life.

**Prayer:** Lord, when we are tempted to give up, or hold onto past hurts, please give us the grace to begin again, so we may live in the freedom and joy of your love. Amen.

# Day 86

*We are all called to be holy by living our lives*
*with love and by bearing witness in everything*
*we do, wherever we find ourselves.*

— *Pope Francis*

We are all called to greatness and to make a difference in this world, but that does not necessitate grandiose measures. We don't have to do great things. We don't even have to do difficult things. The small and simple acts of love we do each day within the home have the power to change the world. We are most tempted to give into our vices with those with whom we spend the greatest amount of time. This is why, with each moment we choose to truly love our spouse and our children, we build a culture of love within our home that ripples outward to the world.

**Prayer:** Lord, help us to love in a way that changes the world. Make our marriage a witness of your love. Amen.

# DAY 87

*Forgiveness is above all a personal choice, a*
*decision of the heart to go against the natural*
*instinct to pay back evil with evil.*

— *Pope St. John Paul II*

To truly forgive goes against our natural inclination. It is a decision we must make. Forgiveness leads to restoration in our relationships and is a vital ingredient in a healthy marriage. The more deeply we love someone, the more pain we feel when we are hurt by them. Do not be afraid to love deeply though, because the deeper we love, the more joy we will experience. Big fish are not caught in shallow waters. Go deep but be ready to forgive. Our emotions can be a barrier to forgiveness. But when we withdraw from or punish someone we love because we feel hurt, we are acting selfishly. True love demands more of us, and Christ Jesus shows us how to set aside our own self-interests and repay evil with good.

**Prayer:** Lord, help us be slow to anger and quick to forgive one another. Amen.

# Day 88

*The woman's soul is fashioned as a shelter*
*in which other souls may unfold.*

— *St. Teresa Benedicta of the Cross*

God created women to be the heart of the home and a shelter for our family. Ladies, do our husbands find shelter in our souls? Is our heart a safe place for him to enter and find reprieve when he feels worn out and weathered? Kathleen yearns for Troy to feel secure and loved when he enters her heart, but she recognizes there have been times when he has avoided it because she selfishly withheld her welcome sign. If we want our husbands to authentically enter our hearts and discover a haven in our love, we must welcome them through our daily actions. It is our duty as wives to create an atmosphere of love in our homes in which our husbands can feel free to unfold, to be who God created them to be.

**Prayer:** Lord, help us to provide a refuge for one another, and to seek that refuge in one another's love. Give us the grace to fulfill our distinct roles according to your plan. Amen.

# Day 89

*If I then, your Lord and Teacher, have washed your feet, you*
*also ought to wash one another's feet. For I have given you*
*an example, that you should also do as I have done to you.*

*— John 13:14–15*

When she was five, our daughter Marianna spent Holy Week in the hospital. She was admitted on Palm Sunday, and for several days the doctors were unsure what was triggering her serious symptoms. Our fear was very real. When Holy Thursday arrived, Troy offered to stay with Marianna, and Kathleen attended Mass with our other children. Troy had been scheduled to have his feet washed during the service that year, but had to cancel due to our circumstances. Kathleen watched the ritual washing and thought about how Troy was truly living the symbolism of the act by serving our daughter at the hospital. Christ's example of washing his disciple's feet demonstrates the value of serving our brothers and sisters with love and humility. It is doing the little things each day for our children, our spouse, our aging parent, our neighbor recovering from surgery, our friend who needs an ear to listen — these are washing the feet of God's people.

**Prayer:** Lord, help us serve one another faithfully each day with sincere love and humility. Amen.

# DAY 90

*If a marriage is to preserve its initial charm and*
*beauty, both husband and wife should try to renew*
*their love day after day, and that is done through*
*sacrifice, with smiles, and also with ingenuity.*

— *St. Josemaría Escrivá*

Do we renew our nuptial love each day? Are we creative with the use of our time, talents, and resources to keep the flame of our love alive and healthy? The love between spouses is unique and irreplaceable. Treat it as such! Impress upon your heart a dignity and respect for the gift of your beloved so when the challenging times come, your focus is not blurred, and your love remains strong. We all go through times when we feel that the "initial charm and beauty" of our marriage has lost its luster. If this is the season you find yourselves in, try sacrificing, smiling, or getting creative. Often, a simple, genuine smile — you know, the kind where your eyes connect, and your heart skips a beat — can do wonders to renew your love.

**Prayer:** Lord, we desire to renew our marital love each day. Assist us, one day at a time, to use well the gifts you have blessed us with, so we can be purposeful and passionate about keeping our love alive. Amen.

# DAY 91

*To receive God's grace, our hearts must be empty*
*vessels and not filled with self-esteem.*

— *St. Francis de Sales*

We can have the best intentions and truly desire to love others well, but still be very full of ourselves. Sometimes this is rooted in our own unmet needs, and sometimes it's just old-fashioned selfishness. It can help to make a habit of asking ourselves, "How empty a vessel is my heart?" Be honest. Do I regularly have to be right? Is the last say consistently mine? Do my actions reflect a heart full of myself and my own needs, wants and desires, or is my heart open to self-giving love? That kind of emptiness is the key to receiving God's grace, not just for marriage, but for every aspect of our lives.

**Prayer:** Lord, please shed light on anything that prevents us from completely giving and receiving authentic love in our marriage. Empty us of selfishness and fill us with your love so we can be a channel of that same love for one another. Amen.

# DAY 92

*Greater love has no man than this, that a
man lay down his life for his friends.*

*— John 15:13*

What a great quote — especially for men! It doesn't take long to
conjure up heroic acts such as those of William Wallace (*Braveheart*), Obi Wan Kenobi (*Star Wars: A New Hope*), Ethan Hunt (*Mission Impossible*), Indiana Jones, James Bond, and countless other men, both fictional and historical. After all, men were born to save the day, protect the damsel in distress, and fight battles in order to secure victory. Yet, these are just acts of physical strength. We do well to consider what Jesus did instead. He saved us all, not through physical acts of heroism, but through a selfless, painful, and humiliating act of love — by laying down his life on the cross. It's important to remember that the most heroic acts are the ones we do with little if any recognition. The greatest love involves laying down our lives.

**Prayer:** Lord, help us lay down our lives for one another each day through small, heroic acts of love. Amen.

# Day 93

*Marriage is good for those who are
afraid to sleep alone at night.*

— *St. Jerome of Stridon*

When we were first married, Kathleen expressed that one of her favorite things was sleeping next to each other. Now, after more than a decade of marriage and five children later, she still says it is one of her favorite things to do! For her, there is truth in Saint Jerome's words. Kathleen's not "afraid to sleep alone," but her heart longs for companionship and a sense of connectedness and security. It does not matter much if you sleep alone. In fact, due to children sharing the bed, a medical issue, snoring, etc., you and your spouse might not sleep together at all for a season of your marriage. What is at the heart of Saint Jerome's words is that each person who chooses to marry experiences a longing for companionship, which brings them together.

**Prayer:** Lord, help each of us discover the truth of why we chose marriage as our vocation and then speak through us as we share our discoveries with one another. Amen.

# DAY 94

*Therefore what God has joined together, let no one separate.*

*— Mark 10:9 (NRSV)*

We struggle with this one daily. With five children ages five to twenty-two, we are regularly tugged in multiple directions and often feel like we are spread too thin. With the myriad of "pulls," we have recognized the need to be decisive and united in our response to them, lest they pull us apart. But resisting division isn't just something we need to practice at home. In our fast paced, media-driven society there are a surplus of outside influences that have the potential to cause division in marriage. And we need to be vigilant. Estrangement usually starts out small, but if we are not attentive and purposeful in our actions, it may steadily grow over time, unconsciously and unintentionally becoming significant. The good news is God's love is the bridge to reunite our souls. If there is any division between us now, we can allow his love to be the magnetic force that draws our hearts back into union by making a commitment to pray together.

**Prayer:** Lord, please give us eyes to clearly see what separates us and the grace and fortitude to root it out of our marriage. Amen.

# Day 95

*Do not forget that true love sets no conditions; it
does not calculate or complain, but simply loves.*

— *Pope St. John Paul II*

Do we love our spouses unconditionally, or do we calculate and complain? True love knows no limit in giving more, being more, forgiving more. For love to be genuine, it must not keep score. We must learn to rise above acting as if there will be a winner and a loser when a disagreement arises. The reality is, we are on the same team in marriage. If one spouse loses, we both lose; but if one wins, we succeed together.

**Prayer:** Lord, please provide us with the grace to love one another without limits, and not to lose sight of the fact that we are on the same team. May our marital love be free, fruitful, selfless, and life-giving. Amen.

# DAY 96

*Therefore a man leaves his father and his mother
and clings to his wife, and they become one flesh.*

— *Genesis 2:24*

While referencing this Scripture, a priest friend jokingly said, "Yes, but the problem is deciding which flesh!" In all seriousness, the molding of two lives into one can be a painful process. Marriage requires a reordering of priorities and loyalties. Anyone who grew up as the center of attention in their home cannot carry this same expectation into marriage. And couples who cling to the security of their past may unintentionally disrespect their marital union in Christ. When it comes to making important decisions, for example, it's important to consider who we listen to more readily: our parents, siblings, friends — or our spouse. While it's fine to seek advice from our family of origin, the feedback our spouse offers should take precedence. There is no room for selfishness in marriage. Imagine how much fruit we could bear as a couple if we really were "one flesh."

**Prayer:** Lord, daily mold our hearts into one. When we are tempted to be selfish, give us the grace to be selfless. When we want to cling to our past securities, help us cling to one another and to you. Amen.

# Day 97

*Commit your work to the Lord,*
*and your plans will be established.*

— *Proverbs 16:3*

God has a plan for your marriage, but so does the enemy. Think about it. Marriage is under attack now more than ever. The very definition of what constitutes a marriage is being questioned and redefined. In the past fifty years, we have progressed in ever-expanding moral relativism with the sexual revolution, abortion on demand, no-fault divorce, and same-sex marriage. We can't even imagine what might come next! There is a battle for truth. Married couples are invited to be a witness to the truth of God's plan. If we desire to have a healthy, holy, and happy marriage, we must put our armor on daily and stay engaged in the battle. Our armor is a profound love for our spouse, which springs forth from a deep commitment to prayer.

**Prayer:** Lord, we firmly believe your plan for our marriage is the best plan. Please equip us with the wisdom, tools, and knowledge to follow it with courage and tenacity. Amen.

# Day 98

*Therefore encourage one another and build
one another up, just as you are doing.*

— *1 Thessalonians 5:11*

The support and encouragement we receive from each other is often what inspires and motivates us to be bold and brave in what we do. Troy is Kathleen's greatest cheerleader, and when she feels down and questions her talents and abilities, he is the first person to remind her of her God-given gifts and purpose for why he has blessed her with them. There are moments when our faith is tested, and we temporarily feel off-balance in our walk with God. In those moments, it is important to know that we aren't walking alone, but together. That is often the best encouragement we can give — or receive!

**Prayer:** Lord, we desire to completely support and love one another. When we are tired, weak, or do not feel like offering encouragement, please give us the strength to provide it. Help us build each other up. Amen.

# Day 99

*Who can find a good wife?*
*She is far more precious than jewels.*
*The heart of her husband trusts in her,*
*and he will have no lack of gain.*
*She does him good, and not harm,*
*all the days of her life.*

— *Proverbs 31:10–12*

In the Old Testament, jewels weren't worn casually. They were extremely rare and valuable, used primarily as a sign of marriage commitment or to adorn royalty or as objects used in worshiping God. Proverbs not only compares a good wife to jewels, but elevates her as "far more precious." When a man finds a "good" wife who both loves God and cares for him, he has indeed found a rare and priceless treasure. But the jewels spoken of in the Bible aren't gemstones; they are virtues. When a woman is virtuous, she is more beautiful than any jewel ever could be. And that is why the heart of her husband trusts in her. We are not meant to focus on lavish external adornments, but on the priceless virtues that shine from our hearts.

**Prayer:** Lord, thank you for the gift of virtue, and for all the precious qualities that empower wives to do good for their husbands, and for husbands to love and trust their wives. Amen.

# Day 100

*To love sovereignly is to love totally.*

— *St. Francis de Sales*

Married couples may, at some point, find themselves in an endless cycle of tit-for-tat: If you do this, I will do that. But God calls us to a higher standard of loving — to love our spouse without measure, without counting the cost, without keeping score, even without expecting anything in return. In order to break the destructive cycle of demanding something in return for our love, we must each die to our own desires and expectations. When each spouse is looking out for the good of the other, real love is exchanged. The more we live this in our marriage, the more deeply loved we will feel. Our motive must be love: love for God and love for our spouse. The bonus is that this behavior is attractive and further motivates us to reciprocate the same kind of love — love without measure.

**Prayer:** Lord, help us love one another selflessly and without measure. Amen.

# DAY 101

*To bear witness to the inestimable value of the indissolubility and fidelity of marriage is one of the most precious and most urgent tasks of Christian couples in our time.*

— *Pope St. John Paul II*

One summer Kathleen took our daughter, Marianna, who was nine at the time, for a little mother-daughter get away at a beach in Michigan. While they were swimming in the lake, Marianna suggested they each list five things they love about one another. "I'll go first mommy," she gleefully exclaimed. "I love that you love Daddy!" Wow! Even though she was young, our daughter communicated a profound truth: The greatest gift we can give our children is to love our spouse.

Our children at every age and stage watch us and often model what they see. When Mom and Dad are united in authentic love, children feel secure. The love we share as husband and wife provides a foundation upon which our children can build and freely grow into the people that God created them to be. To daily deepen the love we have for one another is most certainly an "urgent task."

**Prayer:** Lord, may our love for another bear witness to the indissolubility and fidelity of marriage. Amen.

# Day 102

*Put out into the deep.*

*— Luke 5:4*

There are a lot of unknowns when we get married. We make a commitment to our spouse with little or no knowledge of what lies ahead. It's all these uncertainties, however, that make our marriage vows significant. They are a promise made in a time of joy, meant to hold up when trials come. We may experience wealth, or we may struggle financially. We may be blessed with children or battle infertility. We may enjoy good health or face debilitating illness. All these uncertainties existed on the day we said, "I do," and yet we still took the leap, we still made vows to one another. Love motivates us to move forward in faith. God's love is what allows us to live our vows in confidence, knowing that whatever we experience together as a married couple is part of his plan for our life. That's what makes marriage an exciting adventure we embark on together.

**Prayer:** Lord, thank you for the great adventure of marriage! May we lovingly embrace each season we go through and trust in your plan for our life together. Amen.

# DAY 103

*Christ assigns the dignity of every
woman as a task to every man.*

— *Pope St. John Paul II*

It is a husband's responsibility to help his wife comprehend her incredible worth. A husband's love must speak loudly, clearly, and regularly to her innate dignity as a daughter of God and precious gift. Our self-worth ultimately comes from God, but it is the mission of every man to reinforce the dignity and inner beauty of every woman. We have all had that one friend or family member who only contacts us when they need something from us. This leaves us feeling used rather than valued. A godly man does not use his wife as a means to an end. In a special way, God has called men to protect the dignity of the women in their lives and provide them with a warm, safe, secure, and loving environment where they will never doubt their worth. That begins with cultivating mutual respect in our marriage.

**Prayer:** Lord, may our self-worth founded in you be reinforced daily through our genuine love for one another. Amen.

# Day 104

*Scarcely had I passed them,*
*when I found him whom my soul loves.*

*— Song of Solomon 3:4*

Prime time is not easy to give — our work expects it of us, our children demand it of us, and our goals require it of us. Balancing our time between our obligations and our marriage requires forethought and planning. Our spouse is our soul mate, the one chosen by God to be our path to heaven. There is no relationship more important in our life than the relationship we have with our spouse; therefore, it must take precedence above all else if we want it to mature and flourish. It's important to honestly evaluate how often we give our spouse what's left at the end of the day. How often do we give our spouse prime time when we are alert and able to focus on what they want to share with us? How can we rearrange our schedule to more frequently spend quality time together? Leftovers just aren't as good.

**Prayer:** Lord, help us prioritize prime time with one another as opposed to simply giving whatever we have left at the end of the day. Amen.

# DAY 105

*Pray for me, as I will for thee, that we*
*may merrily meet in heaven.*

*— St. Thomas More*

It is a much better use of time to pray for our spouse than it is to whine about him or her to our friends and family. If we want to meet our spouse in heaven, then we must spend our earth living with that end goal in mind. Too often we complain about what our spouse does and doesn't do that annoys us, rather than shutting our mouths and taking our concerns to God in prayer. It may be tempting to criticize our spouse to others, but this damages our marriage and tempts others to form judgments — usually unfavorable ones — about our spouse. Seeking encouragement from a faithful and trustworthy friend or family member during difficult times is understandable, but it is important to know the difference between complaining and seeking wise counsel. It is even more important to be charitable to our spouse.

**Prayer:** Lord, we desire to live our lives in line with your will so when our earthly marriage ends, we will meet again in heaven with you. Help us to pray for each other and talk with each other more than we talk about each other. Amen.

# Day 106

*The best way to acquire true dignity is to wash*
*one's own clothes and boil one's own pot.*

— *St. Francis Xavier*

In marriage, the best way to acquire dignity — that is, the state or quality of being worthy of honor or respect — is through faithfulness to the everyday responsibilities of married life. A husband and wife give witness to the grace of the Sacrament of Matrimony when, in a spirit of love and service, they embrace each duty they are responsible for in marriage. When we serve our spouse and family in fidelity to our vocation, we are serving God. Our modern culture might have us believe that to become men and women of honor necessitates great measures. On the contrary, it is most often through embracing the mundane, unglorified tasks we do each day that we glorify God and become men and women of authentic dignity.

**Prayer:** Lord, help us embrace the mundane tasks each day in a spirit of love and service. Amen.

# DAY 107

*Jesus does not demand great actions from us,*
*but simply surrender and gratitude.*

— *St. Thérèse of Lisieux*

Gratitude goes a long way in marriage. When we start to become dismayed by the attributes we don't like about our husband or wife, it helps to make a mental list of everything we do like. Express gratitude for the qualities you appreciate. Does your wife take care of the children in the morning so you can exercise? Thank her. Does your husband shovel the driveway after a night of heavy snowfall? Thank him. Expressing gratitude for the good things your spouse does is essential and helps to cultivate a close and rewarding relationship. If something is sincerely bothering you about your spouse, let them know in a loving way. There are qualities and mannerisms about your spouse which carry less weight and have little to no impact on the bigger picture. We must accept and learn to overlook these in order to grow a mature and healthy marriage. Focus and work on what matters most for a strong marriage and learn to surrender all else.

**Prayer:** Lord, fill our hearts with gratitude for the gift of one another and the blessing of our marriage. Give us the wisdom to choose our battles wisely and the grace to let go of things that do not matter. Amen.

# DAY 108

*There are those who seek knowledge for the sake of knowledge; that is curiosity. There are those who seek knowledge to be known by others; that is vanity. There are those who seek knowledge in order to serve; that is love.*

— *St. Bernard of Clairvaux*

Our deepest desire is to be known; in marriage, our spouse should be our chosen field of study! Daily, God invites us to dive deeper into the mystery of our spouse with expectation and enthusiasm. Learning who our spouse is — what he values, what she fears, his struggles, her hopes and dreams — is a lifelong education in the heart and soul of our beloved, and a journey that draws us closer together. Desire to know your spouse even better than you do now. Ask questions and then listen to what your spouse has to share. Safeguard what your spouse tells you and never use your spouse's weaknesses as ammunition. As we uncover more of who our spouse is, we will discover a depth of beauty and significance inside that will amaze us.

**Prayer:** Lord, help us to appreciate the mystery of one another and commit ourselves each day to grow in our knowledge and understanding of the other. Amen.

# DAY 109

*But there is another and interior way of praying without
ceasing, and that is the way of desire. Whatever else you
are doing, if you long for that Sabbath, you are not ceasing
to pray. If you do not want to cease to pray, do not cease
longing. Your unceasing desire is your unceasing voice.*

— *St. Augustine of Hippo*

This is good news! We may long for time alone with God — a private meeting in the chapel — but Saint Augustine assures us that while there is no substitute for prayer, the simple desire to be with God is a form of prayer in and of itself. Our desire and longing for God, lived out through our day-to-day tasks, can become a living prayer. In marriage, we may experience a desire to be together, even when that's not possible or practical. We learn to offer up all we do each day for the greater good of our spousal union and family life. Our longing for God is similar. We may experience the desire to spend time in the intimacy of prayer when the demands of our lives make that difficult. Remember though, that it is our life here on earth, lived out within the vocation of marriage, that is our path to eternal union with God.

**Prayer:** Lord, help us live our vocation each day in such a way that our lives become a seamless offering of prayer. Give us the grace to find opportunities to spend time alone with you and each other. Amen.

# Day 110

*Remember that the Christian life is one of action,*
*not of speech and daydreams. Let there be few words*
*and many deeds and let them be done well.*

— *St. Vincent Pallotti*

The old adage "Actions speak louder than words" applies here. It is good to frequently tell our husband or wife that we love them, but it is far more important for those words to manifest themselves in our daily actions. Do we bear our share of responsibilities each day? Do we follow through on commitments we make? Do we respect our spouse and sincerely listen to what he or she has to say? Do our actions match our words, or do they contradict each other? What we *do* communicates more clearly than what we *say* because it demonstrates our true intentions and feelings. When we do speak, we should be sure to taste our words before we spit them out. Remember that while words can be forgiven, they are not easily forgotten.

**Prayer:** Lord, may our words be few, and our deeds done in love be many. Amen.

# DAY 111

*As to what good qualities there may be in our souls, or who dwells within them, or how precious they are — those are things we seldom consider and so we trouble little about carefully preserving the soul's beauty.*

— *St. Teresa of Ávila*

The strength and depth of our interior life with God will determine how well-equipped and capable we are of living an integrated life as a married man or woman. Our marriages are dependent upon the health of our souls and our ability to maintain inner peace despite whatever is transpiring externally. A few summers ago, our family had the opportunity to travel to Ávila, Spain, home of Saint Teresa. The city is contained within ancient castle walls, and growing up within the walls of a castle is what inspired Saint Teresa to write *The Interior Castle.* In it, she talks about the need to develop an interior life of prayer. It is important for us to take time to develop our interior castle. God longs for us to live as his royal court within the walls of our home. He is the king of our domestic church and we, as husbands and wives, are his princes and princesses.

**Prayer:** Lord, help us continually grow our interior lives, and may our souls be sustained by your peace throughout every season of our marriage. Amen.

# Day 112

*Accustom yourself continually to make many acts
of love, for they enkindle and melt the soul.*

— *St. Teresa of Ávila*

We were attending a parish mission one evening at our church, but because of commitments prior to the event, we drove in separate vehicles. As we left to head home at the end of the evening, Troy gave Kathleen a quick kiss and said, "I love you." Our drive home was short, but after only three minutes, Troy called Kathleen just to say again, "I love you; I really love you." It didn't take much effort, but it spoke volumes about Troy's love. To know that our spouse is thinking about us is one of the greatest feelings in the world. If we are lovingly thinking about our spouse, make him or her aware of it. Send a text, just because. Call for no specific reason. If something triggers a special memory of your life together, share it with your spouse. Little acts of love have great impact.

**Prayer:** Lord, help us not lose sight of the little acts of love we can do each day that breathe life into our marriage. Amen.

# Day 113

*How often I failed in my duty to God because I*
*was not leaning on the strong pillar of prayer.*

— *St. Teresa of Ávila*

There is power in the prayers we pray for our spouse. But this power often calls us to action. What can I change to be a more loving and kindhearted wife? How can I better understand my husband's way of handling this current situation? What does my wife need from me in this moment? How can I best love her right now? When we pray for our spouse, God often places on our heart what we must do and/or change to be the husband or wife our spouse desires and needs. We cannot live the vocation of marriage well on our own power. Instead, we must learn to rely on God's grace and receive it by meeting him in prayer.

**Prayer:** Lord, open our ears and mold our hearts so we can hear your voice. Empower us with your grace to follow your lead. Amen.

# Day 114

*Let the mouth fast from disgraceful and abusive words,*
*because what gain is there when, on the one hand*
*we avoid eating chicken and fish, and on the other*
*hand, we chew up and consume our brothers?*

— *St. John Chrysostom*

One of the surest ways to create tension in marriage is duplicity. A person is duplicitous when his public face does not match his private face. Is the face that everyone outside our home sees the same face that those closest to us at home see? Or do we mask our real selves when in public? It is OK to let our hair down at home, but we must not let go of our virtues. If we live a life of duplicity, we will lose the respect and admiration of our spouse very quickly. God calls us to live a life of both virtue and integrity, and sometimes getting there is a process of growth. We should cooperate with God's grace to be authentic in all our relationships, but especially in our marriage.

**Prayer:** Lord, please help us to live with integrity in all areas of our lives, and to live virtuously at home as well as in public. Amen.

# DAY 115

*Every moment comes to you pregnant with a divine purpose; time being so precious that God deals it out only second by second. Once it leaves your hands and your power to do with it as you please, it plunges into eternity, to remain forever whatever you made it.*

— *Ven. Fulton J. Sheen*

Never miss an opportunity to love. Life is all about the decisions we make from moment to moment, many of which have eternal consequences. Each encounter we have with our spouse has a divine purpose. When we view our marriage through this set of lenses, we become more aware of the impact our words and actions have. In those moments we are tempted to say or text something to our spouse that we know we will later regret, petition God for the grace necessary to love our spouse in that specific moment, regardless of how we may feel. Sacramental grace is ours for the asking. Don't let it go to waste.

**Prayer:** Lord, help us continually live within the grace of our sacrament, so each encounter we have with one another fulfills your divine purpose. Amen.

# DAY 116

*Do you not know that your body is a temple*
*of the Holy Spirit within you, which you have*
*from God? ... So glorify God in your body.*

*— 1 Corinthians 6:19–20*

When we journey through a sickness with someone we deeply care about who has limited time, or when we lose someone we love to death, we acquire a new perspective on life. Daily inconveniences and struggles pale in comparison. After we have journeyed through loss, we understand the value of living like we are dying. God calls us in marriage to live fully and passionately with our end in mind. When we live our vocation each day as if our time is limited and God is going to call us home soon, it changes the entire dynamic of marriage. We don't allow the little things to get us down; we make time for the important stuff; we work at preparing our soul and our spouse's soul for heaven.

**Prayer:** Lord, help us each day to fearlessly and fully live our vocation of marriage with our end in mind. Amen.

# DAY 117

*Hope is the virtue of a heart that doesn't lock itself into darkness, that doesn't dwell on the past, but is able to see a tomorrow.*

— *Pope Francis*

During her sophomore year studying art and English, Heidi began having intense headaches and burning eyes within minutes of beginning to read. She was diagnosed with a rare form of macular degeneration and was bluntly told to "learn Braille and change your major." Heidi slipped into a deep depression. She dropped art, but remained an English major. The next summer, she studied abroad in England. One night in her Oxford dorm room, Heidi struggled to read a book she had been assigned. She heard a knock at her door and a silly voice quoting Monty Python and the Holy Grail. Josh, a student in her program, came to chat about their homework. After Heidi explained her vision challenges, Josh simply said, "Well, I'll read it to you, then!" For the remainder of the summer, Josh read each book assignment to Heidi. Sixteen months after their initial encounter, Josh and Heidi married. After twenty years and raising four children, Josh continues to love his bride by reading to her. The source of Heidi's deepest sorrow, the loss of her vision, gave her husband a vision of how to authentically love her in her deepest need.

**Prayer**: Lord, let the difficulties and sorrows of our lives give us a new vision and inspire us to love one another more deeply. Amen.

# Day 118

*Nothing is more destined to create deep-seated anxieties in people than the false assumption that life should be free from anxieties.*

— *Ven. Fulton J. Sheen*

If we live with the notion that life can and should be anxiety-free, we are setting ourselves up for failure. Most of us know that marriage is not 50/50; it is 100/100. Both husband and wife need to give their all to the marriage if they are going to be successful. Yet even if we both give marriage our all, and together trust in God's plan for our future, this does not make us immune to anxiety. Life will bring many unexpected challenges, and if we don't know how to handle concerns in a constructive way, we may end up burning each other out. The fact is that we all experience some anxiety because our future *is* uncertain, especially when the road together becomes uneven and rough. We must be realistic in our approach to living in our present reality, while trusting in God's divine providence for our future. Unaddressed anxiety doesn't disappear; it deepens. The first thing we can do to prevent that from happening is to accept that we will have our share of worries and commit to handling them together.

**Prayer:** Lord, help us be realistic in our approach to our present reality, while trusting in your provision for our future. Amen.

# DAY 119

*Always try to have success in your work, but*
*remember God is often glorified in your failure.*

— *St. Mary MacKillop*

Kathleen's friend Jessy was visiting in our backyard as our children played. Her son, age five at the time, suddenly yelled for her. Without skipping a beat, she immediately shifted gears from conversation to mom mode. Before she ran over to her son, Jessy said, "My monastic bell is ringing!" When she returned to conversation, Kathleen inquired about her words. Jessy explained that when a monastic bell rings at a convent or monastery, the sisters or monks must immediately stop what they are doing in that moment and go to the chapel. It is an exercise in obedience to the call of their vocation in that moment. As parents and spouses, a child's cry or a spouse's pressing emotional need is our monastic bell. It is through consistent faithful responses to the sounding of our domestic bell that we will be successful in our work within our own little domestic church. Sometimes, despite our best efforts, we fall short in our domestic work. It is in these moments that we should ask God to use our failure for his greater glory.

**Prayer:** Lord, may we faithfully and promptly respond each day to the soundings of our "domestic bell." Amen.

# DAY 120

*To have courage for whatever comes in*
*life — everything lies in that.*

*— St. Teresa of Ávila*

Courage is rooted in deep faith and trust in God's provision for our future as husband and wife, combined with a preparedness for whatever lies ahead. The best way to prepare for the unknown is to start with what *is* known. We know if we put God first and seek his will, then we will have peace whatever may come. We know if we have a strong marriage, then we will weather storms together, as opposed to flying solo. We know if we exercise and eat healthy foods, we are doing what lies within our power to prevent illness. We know if we develop a support system of faithful friends and Catholic community, we will have the strength, stamina, and support to carry our crosses. We cannot predict the future, but we can prepare for it and embrace it with courage.

**Prayer:** Lord, help us prepare ourselves on all levels to faithfully and courageously receive whatever you send our way or allow us to encounter. Amen.

# Day 121

*Torrents of worries and difficulties are incapable of
drowning true love because people who sacrifice themselves
generously together are brought closer by their sacrifice.*

— *St. Josemaría Escrivá*

This quote is one of those marriage ideals we were taught, but until
we personally experienced it in our own marriage, neither of us really grasped it. And now, how we wish we could gift others the deep joy
that comes from two souls sacrificing together for a greater good beyond
themselves. It is life-altering when marriage is actually lived the way God
intends. The word *sacrifice* means "to make holy" (from the Latin *sacer* —
holy — and *facere* — to make). Therefore, each time we sacrifice for one
another or together, we are growing in holiness. Our love for each other
becomes more authentic and further capable of weathering storms with
each sacrifice we make.

**Prayer:** Lord, provide us with the grace necessary to willingly and generously sacrifice of ourselves for one another. Amen.

# DAY 122

*We must be faithful to the present moment or we*
*will frustrate the plan of God for our lives.*

— *Bl. Solanus Casey*

Children will see their share of unhealthy and broken marriages. We can show them that it doesn't have to be that way. We can fight for the "fairy tale" according to God's plan by being faithful to the present moment so as not to disrupt what God wants to do in and through us in that moment. If it is helping clean up dinner, then do it. If it is stopping what we are doing to listen to our spouse share something that is weighing on him or her, then do it. If it is getting out of our warm bed after we have already settled under the covers to ensure the doors are locked, then do it. Life is full of countless small moments of grace that create a beautiful tapestry woven together by the hand of God through our cooperation with his plan for us here and now.

**Prayer:** Lord, may we never underestimate the value of a single moment in union with your perfect will for our lives. Amen.

# DAY 123

*Simply by making us wait, God increases our desire,*
*which in turn enlarges the capacity of our soul,*
*making it able to receive what is to be given to us. So,*
*let us continue to desire, for we shall be filled.*

— *St. Augustine of Hippo*

Across the street from our home is a horse farm. Many days as I am pulling out of my driveway, I am blessed to see the beautiful horses grazing in their pasture. It fills my heart with joy every time. The little things that fill our hearts are God's gifts to us and reminders that he has our lives in the palm of his hand. He gives us just what we need exactly when we need it, and he allows us to suffer just as much as we need to grow in holiness. Sometimes God makes us wait for the things we pray for. But his blessings surround us every day if we simply open our eyes and our hearts to receive them. How does your husband or wife show you God's love? Maybe he brings you coffee when you wake up, or perhaps she cooks your favorite meal. Look for God each day and allow whatever you are waiting for to increase your desire for his active presence in your life.

**Prayer:** Lord, we desire your active presence in our lives. May we seek you each day especially in one another. Amen.

# DAY 124

*Love your wife more than you love your own life. Never
be at odds but be true. Prefer her company at home
above being out. Esteem and admire her publicly and
advise her patiently. Pray together and go to church and
discuss the readings and prayers. If your marriage is like
this, your perfection will rival the holiest of monks.*

— *St. John Chrysostom*

St. John Chrysostom challenges husbands to love their wives more than their own lives, and he provides concrete examples of what that looks like. Ideally, husbands should continually strive to die to their own selfish tendencies. This isn't about giving wives everything they want. As the spiritual head of the home, husbands must be prayerfully aligned with God, so that we are in tune with his will for our marriage. Then, like a knight in shining armor, we lay down our life for our lady, protecting her and helping her grow closer to Christ. We also have an obligation to steer her clear of anything which may take her away from Christ. When a man loves his wife in this sacrificial way, both spouses grow in holiness and virtue.

**Prayer:** (Men) Lord, help me to sacrificially lay down my life each day out of love for you and my wife. May I be the husband you are calling me to be. (Women) Lord, help me to recognize my husband's sacrificial love for me. Amen.

# DAY 125

*Fasting cleanses the soul, raises the mind, subjects
one's flesh to the spirit, renders the heart contrite and
humble, scatters the clouds of concupiscence, quenches
the fire of lust, kindles the true light of chastity.*

*— St. Augustineof Hippo*

Many of the external items that exercise a lot of control in our lives (social media, coffee, dessert, alcohol, eating out, television, etc.) are not needs, but wants. But we have become so accustomed to their daily presence, we often confuse our wants and our needs. Fasting from anything for a set period of time helps us put things in proper context and provides us the mental strength to walk away from them when necessary. Fasting is an exercise in self-control, which is an important virtue for a strong and healthy marriage. Greater self-control leads to freedom from being driven by our passions and provides clarity to separate our wants from our needs. When we have self-control in marriage, we are better equipped to respect our spouse's wants and needs. Being able to say no to ourselves makes it easier for us to say yes to others.

**Prayer:** Lord, please shed light on the areas of our lives where we need greater self-control and please give us the grace to implement a plan of fasting. Amen.

# DAY 126

*Let everything in creation draw you to God. Refresh your*
*mind with some innocent recreation and needful rest.*

— *St. Paul of the Cross*

We recently relocated from the windy city of Chicago to the foothills of the Blue Ridge Mountains in South Carolina. Our initial draw to this area (which was followed by much prayer and discernment) was easy access to God's glorious creation. There is something powerful and invigorating about spending time close to nature. It refreshes the soul and renews the spirit. There is beauty everywhere in creation, and spending time in its presence can do wonders for us as individuals and as a couple. Make sure to take time for necessary rest and recreation so you can hear God's voice and follow his will in your marriage.

**Prayer:** Lord, may we always carve time out to be renewed in body and spirit, so we may be the best version of ourselves for one another. Amen.

# DAY 127

*But rejoice in so far as you share Christ's sufferings, that you may also rejoice and be glad when his glory is revealed.*

— *1 Peter 4:13*

God transforms sand into pearls, caterpillars into butterflies, and coal into diamonds using time and pressure. He does the same with us. God allows the trials, tribulations, and pressures of life to form and mold us. This is hard to remember in moments of pain, but it is the reality of the cross. Our crosses have less merit if we do not allow the weight and pressure of them to transform our heart and cultivate our mind. Likewise, God desires to transform our marriage through the daily difficulties we encounter together. The Sacrament of Matrimony is a powerful force that dispenses the graces we need to fuel us along our journey. God permits or appoints a fire because he alone can bring beauty from the ashes. Suffering burns away what is false in us and brings out what is true. Our deepest marital struggles can prepare us for our greatest calling as a married couple. Pain is always temporary if we both give God permission to accomplish his will through it.

**Prayer:** Lord, please mold and form us through our daily trials and tribulations into a living witness of the beauty of sacramental marriage. Amen.

# DAY 128

*Remember that bodily exercise, when it is well-ordered, is
also prayer by means of which you can please God Our Lord.*

— *St. Ignatius of Loyola*

Creating time for exercise and ensuring that we support our spouse in this same endeavor is important. Beyond the physical benefits, exercise enhances our spiritual life and provides for an overall better quality of life and a more fulfilling marriage. Our bodies are gifts, and we are entrusted with their care. As a married couple, we also have the honor of caring for our spouse's body. The two of us have had to be creative and flexible in order for us both to fit exercise into our busy schedules. But we also try to encourage and motivate one another when one of us is in a slump. Obviously, sickness can happen despite how well we take care of our bodies. But taking care of our health and doing what we can to be strong and stay strong can also be a form of prayer.

**Prayer:** Lord, thank you for the gift of our bodies. Help us to treat them with the respect and dignity they deserve. Amen.

# DAY 129

*For the sake of Christ, then, I am content with*
*weaknesses, insults, hardships, persecutions, and*
*calamities; for when I am weak, then I am strong.*

— *2 Corinthians 12:10*

We believe that God makes good of all things. Whatever we give him of ourselves he can use for his glory. A priest-friend shared a story about a married couple he knew. The wife often burnt the biscuits she made for her husband. The husband's response to his wife's sincere apology for burning his biscuits was always the same, "Honey, I love burnt biscuits every now and then." One night the couple's young daughter said, "Daddy, do you really like those biscuits burnt?" He wrapped his daughter in his arms as he said, "Your mom put in a hard day at work today, and she's really tired. And besides, a little burnt biscuit never hurt anyone!" Our spouse is not perfect, and neither are we. Life is full of imperfect people and imperfect things. Learning to accept our spouse's imperfections and embrace our own is key to creating and maintaining a healthy, fruitful, and lasting marriage. God works through our weaknesses when we allow him.

**Prayer:** Lord, help us embrace and accept that your love is greater than our imperfections. Amen.

# Day 130

*It takes three, not two: you, your spouse, and*
*God. Without God people only succeed in*
*bringing out the worst in one another.*

— *Ven. Fulton J. Sheen*

Marriage is a three-twined rope between you, your spouse, and God. When one of the strands begins to fray, the whole marriage will as well. God must be a welcome guest in every aspect of marriage. As individuals we have a responsibility to grow intellectually, emotionally, and spiritually so the cord of our marriage is strong and cannot be broken. Pray for and with each other. Have discussions about faith. Share with one another how you are striving to live your faith, something new God has taught you, or a moment in which God revealed himself to you. Keep faith alive and let it permeate everything. Do not allow outside influences to weaken the integrity of the cord. Fight to keep the three-twined rope tightly bound together in love.

**Prayer:** Lord, may your love and grace always be interwoven through our lives. Amen.

# DAY 131

*The love of husband and wife is the force
that welds society together.*

— *St. John Chrysostom*

Wow! This is a powerful claim. Do we fully appreciate how the love between spouses is a force so robust, it literally helps "weld" society together? Our greatest source of joy in life comes from loving and being loved. When we deeply love God, we have the capacity to deeply love another person. In marriage, we become a source of God's love for our spouse, one which is hopefully received and, in turn, reciprocated. This exchange of the love of God between husband and wife becomes a tremendous witness to authentic love in action. The stronger our personal love for God, the more solid our marriage will be, and the greater impact our mutual love will have on society.

**Prayer:** Lord, please strengthen our love and be our stability. May we bless others through our example. Help us identify the forces that seek to destroy our bond and give us the spiritual stamina to combat them together. Amen.

# DAY 132

*Let all that you do be done in love.*

*— 1 Corinthians 16:14*

When we prioritize the wellbeing of our spouse, we experience fulfillment, because genuine love leads to true joy. We need not do anything extraordinary to show our love. More often than not, authentic love is realized — and communicated — in doing everyday things in a spirit of love and commitment. God does not love us because we are lovable, but because he chooses to love us despite our unworthiness. In marriage we are to mirror this same type of unconditional love. Genuine love never tires. It is always looking for something more to give to the beloved, for a new way to love.

**Prayer:** Lord, may our love for one another be unconditional, tireless, and without reserve. May our hearts grow to fully love one another the way you love us. Amen.

# Day 133

*Whatever your task, work heartily, as serving the Lord and not men, knowing that from the Lord you will receive the inheritance as your reward; you are serving the Lord Christ.*

— *Colossians 3:23–24*

Kathleen is intensely passionate about what she believes in and has to remember to tone her talk down when she speaks of things that make her blood boil. Recently, when sharing her disbelief over an injustice, Kathleen suddenly realized that she was nearly yelling at Troy. She was expressing how broken and hurt she felt about the situation, but none of it was Troy's fault. Although our fervor may be for a good cause, our message will never be received if we do not speak it with humility and dress it with kindness. It is good to share what we are passionate about with our husband or wife, but we must protect our marriage from mismanaged passion. Bottom line: Our spouse is not our punching bag. When we need to vent, we should do it in a charitable and non-threatening way and learn to be sweet, patient, and humble in the extreme.

**Prayer:** Lord, when we speak of things we are passionate about, help us to do it in a spirit of love and charity. Amen.

# Day 134

*So too the celestial harmony is a mirror of divinity,*
*and Man is a mirror of all God's wonders.*

*— St. Hildegard of Bingen*

A few years ago, we were playing I Spy with our children as we took a leisurely walk around our neighborhood. Although the road was familiar, we spotted numerous things we had never before noticed as we endeavored to play the game. It was amazing how much we had missed on our many journeys up and down this same road. Perhaps it would do our souls good to play this game with God — to slow down and open our eyes so we can "spy" the people, situations, gifts, and crosses that he continually puts right in front of us to get our attention. We are surrounded by things that reflect God's beauty, but we most often overlook that in those closest to us. Imagine if we saw our husband or wife as a "glittering, glistening mirror of divinity"!

**Prayer:** Lord, help us to see you reflected in one another and be in tune with the way you speak to us through our spouse. Amen.

# DAY 135

*Every good endowment and every perfect gift is from above.*

— *James 1:17*

When we first met in college at the University of Notre Dame, Kathleen shared with Troy how much she loved watching the sunset. One night, a few weeks later, Kathleen was dismayed at missing the sunset earlier that evening. To cheer her up, Troy drew her a picture of a sunset — sappy, but oh so sweet! Now that we are married, Troy makes a point of ensuring that Kathleen is able to see the sunset as often as possible. He will often text her a picture of a beautiful sunset from wherever he happens to be, especially when he is traveling for business. In fact, those are often the most meaningful pictures, because it conveys to Kathleen that she is still very much on his mind. It's the little things.

**Prayer:** Lord, help us love big through the little things we do each day for one another.

# Day 136

*May the God of hope fill you with all joy and*
*peace in believing, so that by the power of the*
*Holy Spirit you may abound in hope.*

*— Romans 15:13*

Sometimes we need to slow down and evaluate our life in order to accelerate our life in the right direction. Perhaps we need to shift from criticism to complimenting in our marriage; from contempt to building a culture of appreciation in our home; from taking a defensive stance to taking responsibility for our actions; from withdrawing to avoid conflict to engaging to communicate how we feel. Genuine joy is ongoing when we give our all to the vocation God has given us. Shifting our trajectory to the proper direction can be a massive game-changer for marriage. When we travel through life with a chip on our shoulder, each day becomes a burden to carry instead of a gift to be cherished. Remember that joy is contagious; if one spouse radiates it, chances are the other spouse will eventually catch it also.

**Prayer:** Lord, thank you for the gift of joy! Please help us choose joy each day as our preferred method of travel. Amen.

# Day 137

*Let no evil talk come out of your mouths, but only*
*such as is good for edifying, as fits the occasion,*
*that it may impart grace to those who hear.*

— *Ephesians 4:29*

Troy is one of the most positive people anyone will ever meet. He rarely lets things get him down. While his uplifting demeanor is inspiring and to be commended, it has also been a source of contention through the years. Kathleen tends to see the glass half empty. Therefore, when Troy sees it half full, she sometimes gets annoyed. As might be expected, this creates friction. Over the years, Kathleen has grown to more frequently welcome Troy's positive outlook on various life circumstances, and he has learned to look at certain situations a little more realistically. It's a balance we have worked hard to achieve and one we continually work to maintain. As a result, the overall demeanor of our home is much more joyful than we ever imagined possible.

**Prayer:** Lord, may the words we exchange be pure, uplifting and edifying. Amen.

# DAY 138

*Each one of you has to be God's microphone. Each one of you has to be a messenger, a prophet.*

— *St. Oscar Romero*

St. Oscar Romero is not suggesting we speak through a microphone to get our message across, but rather that we *be* a microphone, and let God speak through us. Does God speak through us to our spouse? Do our actions and words breathe life into our marriage? A microphone has no words, no message, apart from its user. If we are to be God's microphone in our marriage, we must listen to him speak to us in the quiet of our heart. There have been countless moments in our marriage where we have heard God speak to us through one another. The closer we walk with God, the more noticeable his voice is.

**Prayer:** Lord, help us quiet our hearts to hear your voice and be a messenger of your love to one another. Amen.

# DAY 139

*Jesus then took the loaves, and when he had given*
*thanks, he distributed them to those who were*
*seated; so also the fish, as much as they wanted.*

— *John 6:11*

The multiplication of the loaves and the fish demonstrates that Jesus takes whatever we are capable of offering him and turns it into more than enough. With five loaves of bread and two fish — the little his disciples were able to give him — Jesus fed a crowd of five thousand and had twelve baskets full of leftovers! Jesus looked with compassion at the crowds who had come to listen to him. They were tired and hungry and had traveled a long way to be near him. In the same way, Jesus looks with compassion on us when we wholeheartedly give the little we are able to give him and trust him to increase and transform it. What are the five loaves and two fish in your marriage? Whatever it is, give Jesus your meager, humble offering and rely on his provision. Ask him to multiply your efforts to be the best husband or wife you can be, to fill in the gaps where you are lacking, and to nourish your marriage with wholesome spiritual food.

**Prayer:** Lord, we give you all that we have and ask you to multiply our humble offering so we may faithfully live our vocation of marriage. Amen.

# DAY 140

*Do not become alarmed or discouraged that you have*
*failings — and such failings! Struggle to uproot them.*
*And as you do so, be convinced that it is even a good*
*thing to be aware of all those weaknesses, for otherwise*
*you would be proud. And pride separates us from God.*

— *St. Josemaría Escrivá*

Whenever Kathleen travels by plane, she tries to get a window seat. She enjoys looking out the window and viewing life below from a different perspective. Occasionally it is cloudy at take-off but within minutes of rising above the clouds, the sun is shining brightly. Everything looks different. Often in marriage, we too must rise above the "clouds" that keep us from seeing things as they really are. Married life often demands that we make a conscious decision to rise above a situation, to be the better person, let a hurt roll off our shoulders, be light in darkness, find beauty in the ashes, be the voice of faith and reason, love when it isn't easy. The sun is always above the clouds. When we act in faith and have the courage to rise above our own weaknesses and failings, we are often able to see things in our marriage from a different perspective.

**Prayer:** Lord, please help us rise above the clouds in our marriage and see things as they truly are, and not simply what we think they are or want them to be. Amen.

# DAY 141

*Jesus is with you even when you don't feel his presence.*
*He is never so close to you as he is during your spiritual*
*battles. He is always there, close to you, encouraging you*
*to fight your battle courageously. He is there to ward*
*off the enemy's blows so that you may not be hurt.*

— *St. Pio of Pietrelcina*

It is during some of the most difficult seasons in our marriage that we have felt the closest to Our Lord. When things are going well between us, we don't feel the urgency to lean on God as much as we do when we're struggling. We don't always feel God's presence in our life, but we can trust that he is always with us and carries us when we feel we can no longer press on. There have been times when each of us has cried out, "I need you, Lord, I need you." And he was there, always providing us what we needed next to stay faithful to the vows we made on our wedding day. Whether through an encouraging word from a friend, a homily at Mass, an innocent remark from one of our children, or a sincere and loving apology. God was there, ever so close, guiding us forward in faith, helping us fight our spiritual battles.

**Prayer:** Lord, strengthen our trust in you so when the storms come and the spiritual battles hover, we have full confidence in your abiding presence. Amen.

# DAY 142

*The storms that are raging around you will turn out to be for
God's glory, your own merit, and the good of many souls.*

— *St. Pio of Pietrelcina*

Marriage has its fill of clouds and storms. Waiting for the clouds to pass or for a storm to end can test every ounce of our patience; however, God allows the clouds and the storms of life to build our endurance, fuel our spiritual stamina, and ultimately reinforce our marital bond. In our darkest moments, in the midst of the clouds and the storms, Christ, our eternal light, is always present if we allow our hearts and our marriages to be penetrated by his light — his love. Light, no matter how small, will always penetrate darkness. Whatever storms you endure, know that God will use them for good. Be the light of Christ in your marriage, the hope in the midst of the storm, and trust that the sun will shine in God's time.

**Prayer:** Lord, help us trust your plan and strengthen our hope in your promises when the storms of life rage around us. Amen.

# Day 143

*He who walks in integrity walks securely,*
*but he who perverts his ways will be found out.*

*— Proverbs 10:9*

Just as flowers blossom in a garden, virtues grow in the soul. We may struggle with sin and selfishness, but if we truly desire to improve and make a genuine effort to do so, God will do the rest in due time. Similarly, the heart of our spouse will blossom as he or she is loved. It's easy to get caught up in a spirit of criticism. But weeding a garden isn't enough; we must make sure that what is growing there has the sunlight and water it needs. One of the surest ways to do that for our spouse is to cherish them. Cherishing is caring for and protecting someone we love as we would anything of precious value. When we cherish our spouse, we do not take them for granted. We go out of our way to notice the good they do and show them appreciation. That's the kind of love that fosters growth over time.

**Prayer:** Lord, thank you for the gift of each other. Help us not to lose sight of the incredible value each of us has. Show us how to cherish one another in a way that brings each of us into full bloom. Amen.

# DAY 144

*Instead you ought to say, "If the Lord wills, we*
*shall live and we shall do this or that."*

— *James 4:15*

If we had to pick one phrase that we have engrained over and over again into our hearts, it would be, "If God wills it." When we make plans and do our part to put our plans into action, we always recognize that our plans will only materialize if God wills it. Our children have grown up hearing this phrase in reference to all we do. We want them to know and understand that God's plan is always best. Even if it is not what we may want or what we had hoped for, we can learn to trust his plan over our own and his provision over what we think we need. If we push our own plan for our marriage and family, we will never truly be happy. It is only when we surrender to God's plan that we find true joy and fulfillment.

**Prayer:** Lord, help us to daily surrender to your will for our marriage and family. Bring our wills in line with yours. Amen.

# DAY 145

*So God created man in his own image, in the image of*
*God he created him; male and female he created them.*

*— Genesis 1:27*

Once while we were driving to an event, Kathleen asked Troy if he could go into her purse and find her lip gloss. After a few minutes of attempting to locate it, Troy finally gave up and joked that going through a purse was like engaging in an archaeological dig! Men and women see things through a different set of lenses, yet God created and uses our unique attributes as husband and wife to complement one another. Our complementarity is what allows us to shine as a married couple. Further, the divinely willed distinctions between men and women are meant to strengthen our relationship with God and with our spouse. When a husband authentically lives his masculinity, it naturally allows his wife to fully embrace her femininity, and vice versa. The secret to creating a marriage that is rich and deeply satisfying is by embracing the fascinating interplay of a man and a woman loving one another according to God's design.

**Prayer:** Lord, help us to accept and embrace our differences and complement one another with our unique qualities as man and woman so we can show the world the beauty of marriage lived according to your plan. Amen.

# Day 146

*I am the good shepherd; I know my own and my*
*own know me, as the Father knows me and I know*
*the Father; and I lay down my life for the sheep.*

— *John 10:14–15*

A s a senior in college, Kathleen was on a ministry team in which each person was asked to pick one title of Jesus to focus on for the entire year. She chose the Good Shepherd. That year, she heard a number of reasons why we often see pictures of Jesus as a shepherd with a lamb around his neck. One popular explanation was that it was customary for a shepherd to break the leg of a habitually wandering sheep. Then, the shepherd would carry it around his neck so the sheep could feel him, smell him, and learn to trust him enough to stop running off. As it turns out, there is no evidence that such a practice ever existed. And that's a good thing! When we stray away from God and what he desires for us, he does not take our free will away but seeks us out and brings us back. He lays down his life for us, but the choice to follow him — or not — is always ours.

**Prayer:** Lord, thank you for being our Good Shepherd. Help us choose to follow you, to trust you more deeply, and to embrace your will for our lives more fully. Amen.

# Day 147

*Stay with me, and then I shall begin to shine as
thou shinest: so to shine as to be a light to others.
The light, O Jesus, will be all from Thee.*

— *St. John Henry Newman*

When we are driving and look at a side mirror to assess our surroundings, there is often a warning sticker to remind us that "Objects in mirror are closer than they appear." The presence of God in our life can be like this. Jesus is often closer to us than we may think. He is present in every area of our life. In marriage, husband and wife are called to be Christ to one another. His love is meant to shine so brightly through us that our spouse feels the love of God through our love. This is God's design for marriage. We should be so in love with Our Lord that our spouse must seek him in order to truly discover us. There is peace and unity in the home when both the husband and wife operate not only as one flesh, but as two spirits filled with the light and love of Christ for one another.

**Prayer:** Lord, may we reflect you to one another and may your presence be seen and felt through the love we share. Amen.

# Day 148

*Perseverance is a great grace. To go on gaining and
advancing every day, we must be resolute, and bear
and suffer as our blessed forerunners did. Which
of them gained heaven without a struggle?*

— *St. Elizabeth Ann Seton*

Kathleen loves the play *The Jeweler's Shop*, written by St. John Paul II. The story focuses on two young couples, who purchase their wedding rings at a local jeweler's shop. The Jeweler represents God. He attempts to help each couple realize the weight of their decision to marry and the lifelong commitment they are preparing to make. Later, after many years of a struggling marriage, one of the couples is on the brink of divorce. Lies and ultimately an affair threaten to destroy their marital bond. The hopeless wife decides to sell her wedding ring back to the Jeweler. When he puts the ring on the scale, it weighs nothing. The Jeweler tells the wife that neither ring will weigh anything without the other. It is a powerful and unforgettable scene.

Our Jeweler wants our wedding rings to truly be an outward sign of our internal commitment to love our spouse, even when the scale tips and we feel as if we are bearing all the weight of love alone.

**Prayer:** Lord, may our wedding rings always serve as a concrete reminder of the vows we made on our wedding day and that the weight of our love depends on both of us together. Amen.

# DAY 149

*Start being brave about everything!*

— *St. Catherine of Siena*

A lthough a man would like to be a hero to his friends and colleagues, he wants to be a hero to his wife even more. But the call to be brave isn't just for men. Wives have the chance to practice courage too. There is a lot of power in praising and affirming one another, but we easily forget that affirming our spouse is more effective than criticizing and complaining. When we fail to acknowledge a heroic or selfless action, we make it harder for our spouse to be courageous and selfless. It is "braver" to praise and value our spouse than to criticize him or her. Anyone can find fault, but love accepts people where they are while affirming what is good. One heroic moment in an ordinary day is what often turns the tide in a marriage. Keep turning the tide.

**Prayer:** Lord, please help us to be brave enough to set aside criticism and affirm what is good in one another. Amen.

# Day 150

*Let nothing perturb you, nothing frighten you. All things*
*pass. God does not change. Patience achieves everything.*

— *St. Teresa of Ávila*

Patience is a learned skill every couple needs to master if they want a fulfilling marriage. Since it does not come naturally to most people, the more we practice it, the more we will improve. Often the day-to-day stresses of life overwhelm us and leave us with little patience for those whom we love most. We need to accept one another's imperfections, but also be able to recognize the difference between what we should change and what we must tolerate for the sake of our marriage and our own peace of mind.

Impatience often reveals a need to be in control. Are you a control freak? Do you stress out when things don't go according to the plan you have laid out in your head? When you notice that your patience is growing thin, ask yourself what it is that you feel you need to control. If it's only a preference and not a nonnegotiable, let it go for the sake of peace in your home. Patience achieves everything.

**Prayer:** Lord, help us be patient with one another and release our control to you alone to guide us each day in our marriage. Amen.

# Day 151

*Our body is a sacred temple. Our mind is the altar. We
have to take care of them. The body and mind are the
reflection of our soul, the way that we present ourselves to
the world, is a visiting card for our meeting with God.*

— *St. Irma Dulce Pontes*

A college professor we knew shared how his wife would brush her hair and teeth, spray a little perfume on, and greet him at the door when he came home. His wife made it a point to present herself well to him each day. It's easy to let ourselves go — to throw on bulky clothes instead of more fitted ones and to wear the same outfit we did two days ago because it is comfortable. We get busy and focused — and after all, we don't want to be vain, right?

Wrong! Vanity is *excessive* pride in one's appearance or abilities, but taking time to put ourselves together and look nice for one another is actually holy — a simple way we can say that we still care about wowing the one we love. Most of us wouldn't meet friends or business associates without looking our best. Why would we present ourselves to each other with any less care when we can make a gift of ourselves in a more attractive way?

**Prayer:** Lord, may we always strive to look and act our best for our spouse. When we fall into complacency, please help us recognize it. Amen.

# DAY 152

*The heavens are telling the glory of God;*
*and the firmament proclaims his handiwork.*

*— Psalm 19:1*

Nature has much to teach us about how we are designed to live our lives. Each season has its own unique rhythm. As our lives unfold, we develop a more mature appreciation and understanding for not only the natural seasons, but for the seasons of life. We are familiar with changes in the natural world as we transition from one season to the next, but how do we prepare ourselves for changes of seasons in life?

First and foremost, we pray! God is already in the future; he knows the road ahead of us. We ask him to be our travel guide. Second, we listen and learn from others. For every season of life there is someone who has walked the way before us, so we seek out the wisdom they can offer us. Finally, we strive to embrace both the good and the challenging seasons — births, deaths, sicknesses, health, plenty, poverty, youth, old age, promotions, or lost jobs. God is in every season of our life, calling us deeper into his heart and transforming us into the person he has called us to be.

**Prayer:** Lord, as we transition from one season to the next in our marriage, may we always trust in you plan. Amen.

# Day 153

*I need nothing but God, and to lose myself in the heart of Jesus.*

— *St. Margaret Mary Alacoque*

One of the biggest temptations couples fall prey to is placing unreasonable and unrealistic expectations on one another. These are often rooted in the mistaken belief that all our needs can be addressed by one person: our husband or wife. That is simply not the case. Why? First, none of us is perfect or capable of loving perfectly, so the love we both receive and give will not be complete. Secondly, while we may have the sense that we were made for each other, ultimately, each one of us was made by God and for him. We cannot expect our spouse to fulfill us, because only God can. If we look to our husband or wife to fulfill all our needs, we will end up disappointed and frustrated because we are expecting them to give us what only God can.

**Prayer:** Lord, may our expectations of one another be loving and realistic. Amen.

# DAY 154

*If a person is seeking God, his beloved*
*is seeking him much more.*

— *St. John of the Cross*

We all want to feel loved and desired regardless of what stage we are at in our relationship. Just as the Lord continually pursues us, we too are called to pursue our spouse. Many of us complete checklists in countless areas of our lives each day, thinking that they are the path to productivity and efficiency. For certain aspects of our lives they are, but not when it comes to our marriage. A spouse should never feel as if time spent with him or her is just one more item on a to-do list. It's so easy to go through the motions each day without meaning and purpose, but the motive behind the deed and the love put into the action say, "I want to do this. I want to spend time with you, because I truly long to be with you." What if we gave everything in our marriage the same way Christ gave everything for us? Imagine the difference this would make!

**Prayer:** Lord, please help us to live our marriage with purpose and passion and not simply go through the motions each day. Amen.

# DAY 155

*Prayer is an act of love; words are not needed. Even if sickness distracts from thoughts, all that is needed is the will to love.*

— *St. Teresa of Ávila*

Growing old together is an attractive adventure. There is a rare beauty and treasure that can be only discovered and experienced by aging with grace in union with the one whom God gives us to love "till death do us part." Although we may have this incredible vision for our marriage, the pressures of life can cause us to lose sight of the true value of our marital bond. We live in a disposable culture. Most things are not built to last, and many of us don't even want them to last, lest we lose out on the latest and greatest. It can be tempting to transfer this same mentality to our intimate relationships. Refocusing our eyes on the goal, a relationship built to last the test of time, can help us deepen our will to love. When we will to love, we will love one another in a way that endures.

**Prayer:** Lord, if it is your will, may we know the joy of growing old together. Help us to love one another deeper with each passing year. Amen.

# Day 156

*If any man would come after me, let him deny
himself and take up his cross and follow me.
For whoever would save his life will lose it, and
whoever loses his life for my sake will find it.*

— *Matthew 16:24–25*

The night our four-month-old son Dominic died of Sudden Infant Death Syndrome, the nurse placed his lifeless body in Kathleen's arms to hold one last time. She knew in that moment she had come so close to Christ on the cross that he could kiss her. She felt his kiss. No one is exempt from suffering. We all have crosses to carry that vary in size and weight throughout the seasons of our lives. It is our duty and our honor in marriage to help one another carry our crosses. If our husband or wife is going through a particularly difficult time, it is our responsibility to bring aid and comfort. We do not need to have all the answers, nor do we need to fix the situation. We simply need to help bear the weight of the cross. This can be done most importantly through listening to and loving our spouse.

**Prayer:** Lord, help us bear the weight of one another's crosses together, and may our suffering bring us closer to you and to one another. Amen.

# Day 157

*Apart from the cross, there is no other ladder*
*by which we may get to heaven.*

— *St. Rose of Lima*

When John and Amanda's daughter, Elizabeth, was twelve, she was diagnosed with the first of two incurable autoimmune blood diseases. Meanwhile, she developed a staph infection that her medical team did not detect. Eventually, the pain became unbearable, and she was brought to a hospital two hours away. There, doctors discovered she had a massive infection in both legs and immediately prepped for surgery. She was at risk for amputation and might even lose her life. For the next two hours, John and Amanda prayed like never before. Their heavy cross drew their hearts together.

The surgeon was able to save both of Elizabeth's legs, and five years later, a new medical technology put the primary disease into remission. In their thirty-eight years of marriage, Elizabeth's illness was the most difficult thing John and Amanda had to faced. During that season they were emotionally, physically, and financially tapped, but the grace of God was abundant, and it carried them through. The ladder of suffering they climbed together brought them closer to heaven and strengthened their marriage.

**Prayer:** Lord, when we find ourselves climbing a painful ladder, lead us closer to you. Give us the grace to embrace it together. Amen.

# DAY 158

*Jesus looked at them and said, "With men it is impossible,
but not with God; for all things are possible with God."*

— *Mark 10:27*

Have you ever watched a fish swim around in an aquarium? Once when visiting the Chicago Shed Aquarium, we found ourselves mesmerized by two rainbow fish. They both kept swimming in circles around each other, as if they didn't know what else to do, in which direction to head, or what pattern to create. Husbands and wives can sometimes find themselves like these two fish — swimming around each other with no clear direction, purpose, or vision — just simply moving to survive. God wants us to do more than just survive in marriage; he wants us to thrive! Married couples need a clear vision of the direction they are heading together. If getting where you feel called to go feels overwhelming, remember to take one step at a time. Do what's necessary, then do what's possible, and suddenly you will find yourselves doing the impossible.

**Prayer:** Lord, please help us to thrive in our marriage and always be moving forward together in faith. Amen.

# DAY 159

*Preserve the warmth of the family, because the*
*warmth of the whole world cannot make up for it.*

— *St. Charbel Makhlouf*

We all crave love, and it is within the family where love is exchanged, nourished, and communicated in its purest form. Nothing can replace the love a husband has for his wife, a wife has for her husband, or the love they both have as mother and father for their children. In fact, the greatest gift parents can give their children is the gift of their love for one another. When children witness the love we have for one another, they feel secure and wrapped in God's love. As parents, we reflect the parenthood of God to them through our love for one another. Spousal love is a fountain from which children daily draw. When they do not see our love for each other in action, they may begin to doubt God's love for them, and become unsure of who they are and what their purpose is. Marriage is the source of family warmth, and there is nothing that can substitute for the lack of warmth in the home.

**Prayer:** Lord, may the warmth of our love for one another be a witness of your love to our children. Amen.

# DAY 160

*Listen to one another with your ears, eyes, hearts, mouths and the palms of your hands, and keep the roaring of the noise of the world away from your homes because it is like raging storms and violent waves; once it enters the home, it will sweep away everything and disperse everyone.*

— *St. Charbel Makhlouf*

If we want our family to be healthy, then we must spend time together. Family time is an essential factor to creating strong bonds of love within the home. As simple as it sounds, it is often challenging to make time together a reality. Patience and creativity are required to carve out moments just to be together. Dual income households, after-school activities, sports, appointments — all of these and more threaten the well-being of the family if not properly managed. Sadly, shared mealtime is often one of the first things to go, although it should be a focal point of family life. Eating as a family (without smartphones or the television) is one of the greatest ways to build a strong family unit. It is a time to ask questions and listen, a time to learn about each person's day and what may be weighing on their mind. Fight to preserve your family life; it is the greatest gift you will ever have.

**Prayer:** Lord, thank you for the gift of our family. Help us to make spending time together a top priority. Amen.

# DAY 161

*You will have won a great battle if you lose*
*the fear of letting yourself be known.*

— *St. Josemaría Escrivá*

A healthy marriage necessitates both emotional and physical intimacy. They are equally important and are designed to complement one another. Deep emotional intimacy leads to more fulfilling and enjoyable physical intimacy. Emotional intimacy refers to the ability to genuinely connect with your spouse through actions that express vulnerabilities and display a deep sense of trust. This type of intimacy facilitates an authentic sense of security within your marriage to be wholly yourself. A lack of emotional intimacy between spouses can create hypersensitivity and feelings of resentment, isolation, and loneliness. The key ingredient necessary to create and sustain the type of intimacy we all crave is the willingness to be vulnerable. Marriage requires the hard and sometimes painful work of exposing our weaknesses and sins in order to truly love and be loved by our spouse. The more vulnerable we become, the deeper we enter into the heart of our spouse, and the stronger our marriage grows.

**Prayer:** Lord, help us be vulnerable with one another so we can come to truly know each other.

# Day 162

*And every day, when your heart especially*
*feels the loneliness of life, pray.*

— *St. Pio of Pietrelcina*

Sometimes in marriage, we feel disconnected, isolated, and disengaged from our spouse. When Troy feels like we are less intimately connected, he will repeatedly say or text the words, "I miss you" to Kathleen. This is his way of alerting her that he feels emotionally disconnected. That's when we need to shift gears and find ways to devote more time to each other. There are many reasons why couples become emotionally disconnected and feel lonely in their marriage. Often, it's simply because one of them has become preoccupied with a pressing situation. But there are more serious reasons. Perhaps trust has been broken, or physical distance due to work or military service has caused emotional distance. One spouse may be coping with a chronic illness, battling a serious disease, or dealing with depression. When we're lonely, we must find a way to talk with our spouse, let them know how we feel, and do whatever is necessary to strengthen our connection.

**Prayer:** Lord, when we begin to feel disconnected from each other, draw us closer to you in prayer and help us to renew our closeness to one another. Amen.

# Day 163

*Suffering is a great grace; through suffering the soul becomes like the Savior; in suffering love becomes crystalized; the greater the suffering, the purer the love.*

— *St. Maria Faustina Kowalska*

What a beautiful image! Through our suffering love becomes crystalized — that is, it takes precise form. No one wants to suffer, of course. But suffering can be used by God to draw us to himself and bring about a definitive good. He allows the crosses a husband and wife carry together in marriage as a means to draw a couple closer to one another and to deepen their spiritual unity. The love a man and woman share in sacramental marriage becomes crystalized through the difficult moments. The deeper the suffering, the purer the love we and our spouse will share, as long as we work together with God's grace. But it's up to us. We have the choice to waste the suffering we endure or surrender it to God and allow him to create a masterpiece of love through the brokenness of our marital life.

**Prayer:** Lord, may our love become crystalized through the suffering you allow us to experience together as a couple united in sacramental marriage. Amen.

# DAY 164

*You don't know what to say to Our Lord in prayer.*
*Nothing comes to you and yet you would like to ask his*
*advice about many things. Look: take some notes during*
*the day of the things you want to think about in the*
*presence of God. And then go with those notes to pray.*

— *St. Josemaría Escrivá*

Kathleen used to text Troy throughout the day as thoughts, questions, requests, or something she wanted to share came to her. Those texts often got buried among other texts from other people, leaving her frustrated and hurt. Together we eventually found a system that works for us. Now if something is urgent (or Kathleen simply wants to let Troy know she is thinking of him), she will text him right away. But if it can wait, she makes a note of it to share with him at a mutually convenient time. Prayer, too, can take place anywhere and at any time. But when there are specific things weighing on us, it is often good to write them down (or take notes on our phones) and use them as a prayer plan. Writing down what we want to say to God keeps us focused on our long-term vision of heaven.

**Prayer:** Lord, help us develop a plan to stay connected to you and to each other throughout the day. Amen.

# DAY 165

*If we wish to make any progress in the service of God, we must
begin every day of our life with new eagerness. We must keep
ourselves in the presence of God as much as possible and have
no other view or end in all our actions but the divine honor.*

— *St. Charles Borromeo*

In many areas of the world, Catholic churches are located in the center of town. It's a powerful symbol of how all life revolves around Christ. When our lives are centered around Christ, our faith informs our decisions, and God's plan for us unfolds in the way he uniquely intended for us. Unfortunately, many people try to fit God into their lives like a mismatched puzzle piece and only when it's convenient or they feel like they need him. This is not how we were created to live. God is the author of life, and he is creating a picture of his love through our marriage. Although it may seem perplexing at times, he has a specific plan for the pieces of our married life to fit together, but he must be at the center of our marriage for all the pieces to fall into place. So let's not force pieces to fit where we want them, but allow God to arrange them by aligning our marriage with his will.

**Prayer:** Lord, help us to make you the center our lives and build our marriage around you so we can live in the freedom of your perfect plan. Amen.

# DAY 166

*In time of desolation, we should never make any change, but
remain firm and constant in the resolution and decision which
guided us the day before the desolation, or in the decision
to which we adhered in the preceding consolation. For just
as in consolation the good spirit guides and counsels us, so
in desolation the evil spirit guides and counsels. Following
his counsels, we can never find the way to a right decision.*

— *St. Ignatius of Loyola*

When we are emotionally drained, it is never a good idea to make important decisions or say important words. Satan waits for our weak moments to make his moves, especially to attack a marriage. Don't give into the temptation to make hasty decisions driven by emotions, but be wary about the ability to think clearly in the moment. It is critical to recharge ourselves physically, mentally, and spiritually before we implement choices that can have life-altering consequences. Wait on God to refresh you so you can be open to the Holy Spirit's lead.

**Prayer:** Lord, please guide us in all our decisions and may your Holy Spirit work in and through us to do your will alone. Amen.

# Day 167

*There must be no hostility in our minds, no*
*contempt in our eyes, no insult on our lips.*

— *St. John Bosco*

Forgiveness is an essential element for a healthy and vibrant marriage. Practicing forgiveness allows us to let go of toxic hurt and shame that would otherwise eat away at our relationship. Forgiveness is a choice regardless of whether an apology was offered. At times, we may want to harbor anger and make our spouse "pay" for causing us pain. But when we choose to forgive, we free ourselves of hostility and can begin to work through the effects of the wound in a healthy manner. And when we are in the wrong and an apology is in order, we should de-weaponize our apology and make it sincere. There is no room for hostility, contempt, or insult in a loving marriage.

**Prayer:** Lord, help us recognize when we are wrong and have the courage to apologize. Please give us the grace to practice mercy in our marriage. Amen.

# Day 168

*Your word is a lamp to my feet
and a light to my path.*

— *Psalm 119:105*

For many of us, prayer is simply a time when we rattle off words we have memorized or read off a laundry list of requests. When we do that, we do not allow God to speak to us. We make it difficult for him to get a word in edgewise! Similarly, the biggest communication problem in marriage is that we do not listen to our spouse to understand what they are saying, but instead listen to reply. Understanding goes deeper than knowledge. We may know that our wife or husband is having a difficult day, but understanding why is another matter. There are many people who know us, but few who understand us. Our spouse's heart is a treasure, a mystery to be uncovered more and more each day. In order to create a vibrant and beautiful life together, we must understand one another. Understanding our spouse is a quest for which each of our hearts was made. We discover the purpose and mission for our marriage by listening.

**Prayer:** Lord, help us to truly listen to you and to each other so we can grow in understanding. Amen.

# DAY 169

*Aspire not to have more, but to be more.*

— *St. Oscar Romero*

Most of the connections we make with people each day are consumer interactions, whether we're shopping for clothes or groceries or various services. When we apply this same mentality to our relationships, we are setting ourselves up for failure. If we aren't careful, we can bring a consumer mindset into our marriage and family life. When our children make the honor roll or excel in sports, we feel proud. If our spouse earns a high salary or a promotion, that can make us proud, too. But what if our children's achievements are average, or our spouse works hard but we don't have a lot to show for it? We can never allow our love or affirmation to be determined by performance or success. What is most honorable and worthy of praise is a spouse who seeks to be more rather than acquiring more material things or accomplishments.

**Prayer:** Lord, help us each aspire to be more rather than to attain more. Amen.

# Day 170

*Above all hold unfailing your love for one another,*
*since love covers a multitude of sins.*

— *1 Peter 4:8*

God wants us to use the ordinary moments of each day as opportunities for extraordinary grace. That includes all our aggravations! The most important work we will ever do is with the people we love most. The family is a school of love where we cultivate relationships and grow in holiness. It is so easy to lose our focus and get distracted by the work we do outside our home and by the annoyances and worries we experience inside the home. If we respond to the everyday difficulties we face with gentleness, patience, and kindness, we will grow in holiness. The choice is ours.

**Prayer:** Lord, thank you for the school of love I have in my family. Help me to receive the ordinary difficulties of each day as opportunities to grow. Amen.

# DAY 171

*Do not put off till tomorrow the good you can
do today. You may not have a tomorrow.*

— *St. John Bosco*

The crosses we are given to carry in life often form wounds that affect the manner in which we respond to certain situations, for good or ill. Our son Dominic died suddenly of SIDS at four and a half months of age. Kathleen had no idea when she laid him down on that warm summer evening that she would never feel the warmth of his body in her arms again. Dominic's death shook us both to the core and has given us a greater appreciation of each moment we have together. None of us leave the house without saying "goodbye" and "I love you." We make it a point to let each other know each day how much we love one another. These are positive fruits from a painful loss. We are never guaranteed another tomorrow with the people we love. Don't go to bed angry. Don't let your husband or wife walk away from you feeling unloved and unappreciated. Focus on the good, and don't put off the love you can show today until you "feel" like loving.

**Prayer:** Lord, help us to not put off until tomorrow the good we can do today, especially in our marriage. Amen.

# DAY 172

*So true is it that misfortune binds hearts together.*

— *Mother Theodore Guerin*

Adversity uncovers our weaknesses. It can expose a lack of trust for our spouse, a need to communicate more clearly, or our own selfish tendencies. When faced with a difficulty, we can choose to blame our spouse and see only their flaws, or we can ask God to reveal our own need for healing. But adversity can also reveal the beauty within our spouse in a new light. When we see how they react and handle a challenging moment with grace, it increases our love for them. Because adversity drives married couples to their knees in prayer and forces them to work together and learn how to better communicate, it has the potential to bind a husband and wife together like no other life experience can. Strong marriages, however, rely on God for restoration. Those couples who attempt to overcome adversity by their own will and strength often find themselves even more divided in the end.

**Prayer:** Lord, use the difficulties we encounter to bind our hearts together. Amen.

# DAY 173

*For true hearts there is no separating ocean.*

— *Mother Theodore Guerin*

I magine if two capsules were dropped in the ocean at the same time in the same exact location and left to float as they may. The chances of them remaining together are slim unless they form a connection that is strong enough to keep them from drifting apart. The two capsules may resurface in entirely different parts of the world because of the vastness of the ocean and the currents that carry them. Husbands and wives are like these two capsules. We start out together united and strong, but if we do not purposefully continue to strengthen our bond, it weakens, and over time the pressures of the world and the currents of life may cause us to slowly drift apart. The grace of our sacrament knows no boundaries and has the power to reunite us even if it seems we are oceans apart.

**Prayer:** Lord, during the seasons of life where we may drift apart, please draw us back together through the grace of our sacrament. Amen.

# Day 174

*Be careful not to give way to your temper, which
makes you unsupportable. You would be a
thousand times happier in resisting it.*

— *Mother Theodore Guerin*

Early on in our marriage, Kathleen was habitually relentless in her attempt to win an argument. This only prompted Troy to shut down. Whether she was right or not, she would have been a thousand times happier if she had simply done what was necessary to put a lid on her fiery temper. When we emotionally shut our spouse down, it initiates a vicious cycle that must be broken before both spouses are capable of emotionally engaging again. When we find our feelings brewing to the point of eruption, we should give ourselves permission to take a timeout to calm down, so when we reenter the conversation we can speak clearly and rationally. An argument avoided is better than an argument won.

**Prayer:** Lord, help us to resist our temper flare-ups when we disagree and choose to disengage rather than hurt one another. Amen.

# Day 175

*O Master, make me chaste, but not yet!*

*— St. Augustine of Hippo*

We can all relate to this prayer of Saint Augustine in one way or another. We know we need to change something about ourselves in order to be a better person and have a richer and more fulfilling marriage, but we want God to do it on our schedule, not his. It's not easy to let go of our vices and embrace a more virtuous life. But we will never make progress in our marriage unless we empty our closet of junk and let God's grace flood the areas of our life that need healing. Perhaps there is just that one vice we can't let go of. Perhaps our spouse doesn't even know about it! The reality is that even if a spouse is unaware of a particular vice we struggle with, it still affects the marriage. Marriages grow in grace and experience the peace we all seek only when we come clean. Our attachment to sins and vices always compromises the bond we are building with our spouse.

**Prayer:** Lord, purify us, so we can daily grow in grace and virtue. Amen.

# DAY 176

*Gratitude is the first sign of a thinking, rational creature.*

— *Bl. Solanus Casey*

Sometimes we just have an off day. We may say something we don't mean or do something out of the ordinary. Perhaps we didn't get enough sleep, we feel overwhelmed at work, or we received bad news. Off days are normal, and when our husband or wife is having one, we need to be considerate toward what our spouse may be going through. We should do our best to practice mercy, give our spouse the benefit of the doubt, and not make things worse by feeding into the situation with our own bad attitudes. When we find ourselves harboring negative thoughts, we should remember what we are grateful for in our spouse. Focus on the good and remember that this too will pass. Tomorrow is a new day.

**Prayer:** Lord, help us to maintain our gratitude for one another, especially when we are struggling. Amen.

# Day 177

*Everyone needs half an hour of prayer every day.*
*Unless you're busy. Then you need an hour.*

— *Attributed to St. Francis de Sales*

Ironically the more we have on our plate, the more we need to make sure we are well-nourished spiritually. None of us can give what we do not have or draw water from an empty well. Family life is busy; there is always somewhere to be and something that needs to be done, so making time for prayer is all the more essential to stay on track. Ironically, when we put God first by spending time with him, he gives us all the time we need back. It might be easier just to do our duties in a spirit of prayer rather than carving out time to silence our heart and let God speak to us. But it won't be long before we will be void of the spiritual stamina necessary to do God's will with a joyful heart. While it is good to make your life a prayer and an offering to God, there is no substitute for setting time aside, free from distractions, specifically for conversation alone with God. In fact, the busier we are, the more we need to pray!

**Prayer:** Lord, as I serve my spouse and my family throughout the day, may I do it in a spirit of prayer. Amen.

# Day 178

*Prudence is the knowledge of what to seek and what to avoid.*

— *St. Augustine of Hippo*

Have you ever accidentally touched a hot stovetop just after you'd turned it off or, worse, while it's still on? Ouch! You undoubtedly learned to be more attentive the next time. Conversely, what about when you did something nice for a neighbor in need? You probably felt good inside and encouraged to show kindness again. In each of these two examples, your experiences gave you the knowledge of what to avoid and what to seek in the future.

Saint Augustine reminds us that if we know something is good for us, we ought to keep doing it; and if we know something is bad for us, we should stop doing it. The real challenge comes when something seems to be good, but isn't, or when something appears to be bad, but is good. Prudence helps us to tell the difference. It's a compass which corrects our course toward heaven.

**Prayer:** Lord, help us learn from our experiences. Please give us the gift of prudence so that we can choose what is truly good for us. Amen.

# Day 179

*Do not pray for easy lives; pray to be stronger people. Do not pray for tasks equal to your powers; pray for powers equal to your tasks.*

— *Bl. Solanus Casey*

Champions don't wait for praise or spotlights; they just work to perform everything with excellence. But the ability to excel doesn't just happen; it is the result of perseverance and many unseen sacrifices. Every married couple wants their marriage to thrive. So why don't more couples achieve this goal? The answer is simple: Few are willing to pay the price. The sacrifices we make, the hard work we put in, the late nights and early mornings that no one sees, these are what make us champions and allow our marriage to thrive. Excellence is born out of sacrifice. If we desire to build a strong marriage, we shouldn't fool ourselves into thinking that we can look for the easy way out of our challenges. Instead, we should expect to put in the work behind the scenes and pray for the grace to match our tasks.

**Prayer:** Lord, give us the grace to make our best effort and the willingness to sacrifice what is necessary to cultivate a fruitful and successful marriage that aligns with your will. Amen.

# Day 180

*Why do you see the speck that is in your brother's eye,*
*but do not notice the log that is in your own eye?*

— *Matthew 7:3*

Why is it so easy to notice "the speck" in our spouse's eye, instead of recognizing "the log" in our own eye? Since we live and interact with our spouse daily, we can be quick to notice what they do wrong instead of focusing on what they do right. Kathleen has been humbled time and again after pointing out a fault to Troy and then realizing that she has done something equally annoying that he never said a word about. The key is to work on our "log" instead of focusing on the things we might feel need some attention in our spouse's life. When we each take responsibility and do what we can to improve ourselves the whole world changes for the better.

**Prayer:** Lord, help us focus on what needs attention in our own lives so we can live a healthy and dynamic marriage. Amen.

# DAY 181

*It must be that you depend on the "lay apostles" to
bring the celestial fireworks into the market.*

— *St. Katharine Drexel*

People are hungry for authentic examples of love. We are called to evangelize the world through our vocation of marriage. God has entrusted this important mission to each of us, and he depends on us to reveal his love to others through our love for our spouse. Fairy tales and romance movies should pale in comparison to the reality of sacramental marriage! Christ will be exalted in our marriage as we follow him into abundant living as a married couple. He intends our marriage to be so healthy and secure that it shouts to the world the real meaning of love. We may not realize it, but the world is watching and wondering whether the reality of Jesus as Lord makes a difference in our marriage. They want to know whether God really is good and worthy of their commitment. The depth of our trust, the level of joy and respect they see in us as a couple, and the intensity of our commitment to one another may be the only window others have to see God's love and his plan for their lives.

**Prayer:** Lord, may our marriage be a witness to the world of the power of your love. Amen.

# Day 182

*You pay God a compliment by asking great things of him.*

— *St. Teresa of Ávila*

We also pay our spouse a great compliment when we ask great things from him or her. This is not to diminish the faith God wants us to have in him. Rather, it is our honor and responsibility to support, compliment, and encourage our beloved. When we wholeheartedly believe in our spouse, it fuels them to be the best version of themselves. We know our spouse better than anyone; therefore, when we have confidence in their abilities, it speaks volumes about the truth of who they are and what they have to offer.

**Prayer:** Lord, may we always support, encourage, and wholeheartedly believe in one another and our unique abilities to do great things. Amen.

# DAY 183

*The way Jesus shows you is not easy. Rather it is like a path
winding up a mountain. Do not lose heart! The steeper
the road, the faster it rises towards ever wider horizons.*

— *Pope St. John Paul II*

In May 2017 our family was blessed to travel to Europe for a three-week vacation and pilgrimage. We toured four different countries in a rented van. When we crossed the border from Spain into Andorra, we were already at a high altitude, but little did we know at the time that our ascent was just beginning. We drove higher and higher with no guardrails. It was terrifying and thrilling at the same time. The views were absolutely astounding, but it required incredible trust in God's provision. That ascent in Andorra is now one of our fondest family memories.

God gives us a road map to follow in sacramental marriage through the beautiful teachings the Catholic Church lays out for us to embrace. If we follow God's plan for marriage and trust him throughout our journey of twists and turns, we can be assured of incredible vistas along the way and a destination that is beyond what we can imagine. We cannot always see the road ahead, but we can choose to move forward in faith.

**Prayer:** Lord, help us trust the plan you have for our marriage and walk forward in faith each day. Amen.

# DAY 184

*I appeal to you therefore, brethren, by the mercies of*
*God, to present your bodies as a living sacrifice, holy and*
*acceptable to God, which is your spiritual worship.*

— Romans 12:1

One of the most beautiful gifts we can give our spouse is willingly making sacrifices for their intentions. Is our spouse struggling with a particular challenge? We can offer our daily inconveniences and struggles up for them. When we do this, it takes our focus off ourselves and puts it on our beloved. A healthy marriage will include sacrifices for each other. Are we willing to give up "me time" in order to care for a sick husband or wife, or work extra hours to make something that's important to him or her a reality? How about getting up with the children in the morning and letting our spouse sleep in? Marriage offers ample opportunities to cultivate the kind of love that can make sacrifice a joy.

**Prayer:** Lord, give us the grace necessary to be willing to offer our daily sufferings for our spouse's needs and intentions. Amen.

# DAY 185

*The sin of the century is the loss of the sense of sin.*

— *Ven. Pope Pius XII*

One of the most difficult crosses to carry in marriage is taking responsibility for how our own sinfulness hurts our spouse, and waiting patiently for our spouse to do the same. It's important to remember that all of us have blind spots, and we all sin. Sometimes nothing we say or do will have much impact. Love, however, always does. When one of us sins, we've found that the best response is to communicate the truth in a gentle way, and then let go of it. Once we forgive our husband or wife, we can pray that God will open their eyes and give them the grace to recognize their sins and any hurt that has been caused as a result. Remember, though, that this is a two-way street. We can't be pointing out our spouse's sins and be unwilling to acknowledge our own.

**Prayer:** Lord, help us to truly know ourselves and have the humility to recognize when we have sinned. Give us the grace to see one another's weaknesses as opportunities for forgiveness. Amen.

# Day 186

*We must learn to live together, to understand one another, to make allowances, to be brotherly and, at times, in the words of Saint John of the Cross, "where there is no love, put love and you will find love." We have to do this even in the apparently uninspiring circumstances that arise in our professional work or in our domestic and social life.*

— *St. Josemaría Escrivá*

A few years ago, we both ended up in physical therapy at our chiropractor's office at the same time, unplanned. We had been in a serious car accident several months before, and the injuries we each sustained required therapy, but we never arranged our visits at the same time. On this particular day, Troy was added in at the last minute. He was unaware that Kathleen was at the office receiving therapy. When she walked into the physical therapy room, she caught Troy out of the corner of her eye in a side room right as he had just completed an ultrasound treatment. What struck us was how excited we were to see each other. We can get so used to the ordinary moments together as a married couple that we sometimes take one another for granted. The genuine delight we both shared, running into each other unexpectedly, brought us joy.

**Prayer:** Lord, help us build a marriage that still makes our hearts flutter after years together. Amen.

# Day 187

*Disorder in society is the result of disorder in the family.*

— *St. Angela Merici*

There is an order to married life that must be followed if we desire to have peace in our home and produce fruit in our marriage. God first, marriage second, family third, work fourth. When priorities are lived out of order, disorder and chaos result, and our married life becomes twisted and complicated. Our jobs are at the service of our family. We should work in order to live, but so often we live in order to work. Children will push to be first, but our marriage needs to come before our children, giving them the security of having parents who deeply love one another. The greatest gift we can give our children is to have a healthy and holy marriage. Nothing else compares. If we place our spouse before our relationship with God, we will eventually end up disappointed and frustrated. When we put God first, we become capable of loving and honoring our spouse despite our imperfections.

**Prayer:** Lord, help us keep our priorities properly ordered so we can have peace in our home and yield fruit in our marriage. Amen.

# DAY 188

*Know thyself and thy faults and thus live.*

— *St. Augustine of Hippo*

Saint Augustine got it. He understood that to be free to truly live we need to know our authentic selves. That includes not only our strengths, but the weaknesses we are often tempted to hide. Do we know our own faults? We can only grow strong if we actively work on our weaknesses and live in a way that takes them into account. But we can only do that if we know what they are. In marriage two become one, and this molding of two lives into one can often be painstakingly slow because one spouse or the other does not know their true identity in Christ. To live the Sacrament of Matrimony in its fullness necessitates a full knowledge of self by both spouses — strengths, weaknesses — the entirety of the gift we are.

**Prayer:** Lord, shine your light on our strengths and on our weaknesses. May we always find our true identity in you. Amen.

# DAY 189

*A single act of love makes the soul return to life.*

— *St. Maximilian Kolbe*

During a rather tumultuous and painful season in our marriage, Kathleen often felt like a droopy flower left unwatered for days on end. Then, just as she was about to die from lack of water (love), Troy would swoop in and give her just enough to keep her alive. Of course, he also felt malnourished during that difficult period as Kathleen's love was not given freely, either. We eventually emerged, and our marriage was brought back to life by many single acts of selfless love over time. During challenging seasons, it's good to remember that we have no control over what our spouse does, but we do have complete freedom to love him or her unconditionally. It often only takes one single act of sincere love to re-ignite the marital flame.

**Prayer:** Lord, help us to pour love into one another so our marriage can grow and thrive in all the ways you desire. Amen.

# DAY 190

*I tell you that you have less to suffer in following the*
*cross than in serving the world and its pleasures.*

— *St. John Vianney*

The natural human inclination is to avoid suffering at all costs: to do all we can to fix what's broken, to medicate sickness, and to numb pain. It's a paradox of the Christian life that we are called to embrace suffering. It's not that we ignore what's broken, but rather, we bring the brokenness to God. Medication is necessary, but it must not be overused or abused. And we must allow pain into our lives, if we desire to truly open ourselves up to others. We often buy into the lie that the pleasures of this world offer us more than embracing the inevitable everyday crosses in marriage with the grace of our sacrament, because the joy and satisfaction that comes as a result is not immediate. It is not that we should go looking for suffering, but, when presented with a cross to carry, we are called to embrace it in love and allow it to form our character.

**Prayer:** Lord, teach us to seek our joy and fulfillment in you. Show us how to embrace the little crosses each day with the grace of our sacrament so we may experience true joy and fulfillment. Amen.

# DAY 191

*And he sat down and called the Twelve and he said to them, "If any one would be first, he must be last of all and servant of all."*

— *Mark 9:35*

A few years ago, Kathleen's friend came to the door wearing an apron. Kathleen commented about how cute it was, and her friend's response was not what she expected to hear: "I wear my apron all day as a reminder that I am called to serve my family in all I do, and it is an honor." Her remark inspired Kathleen that day, and she has never forgotten it. It's far easier for most of us to help the needy old man in the back of church — or even to travel to another country — than it is to serve the people we know best. Why? Perhaps because there is not much glory or immediate reward for our efforts. At home, we strengthen our marriage and family over time as we grow in holiness through the countless ways we care for the needs of our family. Our reward is the love we cultivate within our home.

**Prayer:** Lord, may we always serve those closest to us with a true servant's heart and not count the cost, but rather trust in the eternal value of our daily actions done in love. Amen.

# DAY 192

*By this all men will know that you are my*
*disciples, if you have love for one another.*

*— John 13:35*

What we love drives us, and it is often quickly evident to those with whom we interact. Over the years we have had people comment from time to time about how much we love one another. It is not that we go around announcing our love, but because it is clearly visible. When asked to do something, our typical response might be, "Let me check with Kathleen (or Troy) and get back to you." A simple reply, but one that communicates mutual respect and love. When we interact with others that don't know us, does our behavior reflect that of a married man or woman? Would people know we are married without seeing a wedding ring? Our behavior should reflect the vocation we are living at all times. If we truly love our spouse, we will grow to resemble marital love.

**Prayer:** Lord, may our love for one another be evident to others. May we continually grow to resemble marital love in every aspect of our lives. Amen.

# DAY 193

*When one loves, one does not calculate.*

— *St. Thérèse of Lisieux*

It can be tempting to live marriage in a tit-for-tat state of mind. But if we do, we develop an endless cycle of "calculating" the "cost" of what we do for our spouse. When our love is free, however, it is fruitful, and our spouse feels deeply loved. The times we have fallen into the trap of loving one another with the expectation of getting something in return, our marriage felt more like a business partnership than a sacrament. That's because if we sense the love we are being offered is like checking something off a to-do list, or a claim to receiving something from us, we are unfulfilled. Authentic love is fulfilling — it fills us full, both when we give it and also when we receive it. This is the attractive nature of genuine love. God calls us into relationship with him, so we can learn how to love as he does. The love he gives us is total and selfless. We are called to do the same for one another in marriage.

**Prayer:** Lord, teach us how to love freely and not count the cost or expect anything in return as we love one another. Amen.

# DAY 194

*When you encounter difficulties and contradictions, do not
try to break them, but bend them with gentleness and time.*

— *St. Francis de Sales*

It was 3:00 p.m. on a Monday when Troy called to tell Kathleen that he
had to catch a flight to New York for business at 6:00 a.m. the next day,
and wouldn't return home until Friday evening. This trip was nowhere
on our radar, and the sudden change of plans threw Kathleen into a bit of
a tizzy. Troy has always traveled a lot for work, and often without much
notice, but usually more than twelve hours! Although she knew it was
not his fault and didn't blame him for the news, Kathleen's initial negativ-
ity hurt him. Flexibility is key to sustaining a healthy and holy marriage.
We must be willing to change our ways of seeing things, our ways of handling things, and our expectations. So how do we become more flexible?
We stretch our minds by mentally preparing for whatever change comes
our way, and we stretch our spiritual muscles through prayer. This way
when change inevitably comes, we bend but don't break; we change direction, but we don't get off course; we adapt instead of putting up a fight.

**Prayer:** Lord, help us be flexible each day to accommodate whatever you
send our way. Amen.

# DAY 195

*I frequently feel that certain persons are praying for*
*me. I experience this suddenly in my soul, but I do not*
*always know which person is interceding for me.*

— *St. Maria Faustina Kowalska*

Do you ever sense that your spouse is praying for you? To be uplifted by the power of our spouse's prayers for us is one of the most beautiful feelings this side of heaven. This is not to say that we will always experience this gift, but rather to understand that when we are spiritually connected as husband and wife, there are moments in which our prayers for one another can be deeply felt. We often hear of how Saint Monica prayed for the conversion of her son, Saint Augustine. But Monica also prayed for the conversion of her pagan husband, Patricius. Her prayers for him were also answered, and Patricius became a Christian. There is no doubt Patricius' conversion was a direct result of Monica's years of heartfelt prayers for him. Whatever your circumstances are as a couple, never underestimate the power of your prayers for one another.

**Prayer:** Lord, may we never lose sight of the power of prayer for one another. Amen.

# Day 196

*Husbands, love your wives, as Christ loved the*
*Church and gave himself up for her.*

— *Ephesians 5:25*

Men, just as Christ loves the Church and died for her on the cross, we are called to die to our own selfish desires each day for the sake of our wives. Some days will be easier than others to ignore the daily temptations of the flesh and the world for the sake of prioritizing our marriage. Sometimes, this lofty calling may require heroic measures, and other times it may flow naturally and with little effort. The deeper our love for God, the deeper our love will be for our wife and the more natural it will feel to respond wholeheartedly to love her as Christ loves the Church. The ability to sacrifice our own wants and needs for the greater good of our marriage is empowered through regular time spent with God in prayer. This is where we will find the strength to lovingly live our calling as husbands.

**Prayer:** Lord, help us daily give ourselves up in love so our marriage can fully live and thrive. Amen.

# DAY 197

*Perfect love means putting up with other people's shortcomings,*
*feeling no surprise at their weaknesses, finding encouragement*
*even in the slightest evidence of good qualities in them.*

— *St. Thérèse of Lisieux*

When we were on vacation a few years ago, there was a wood carver hired for entertainment at our resort. Each day he would chisel away at this large chunk of wood. Over the course of the week, we watched the transformation from a piece of wood to a splendid flower. God is our master wood carver. When we permit him, he chisels away at each of our defects so he can make us the beautiful masterpiece he intended us to be all along. In marriage we are privileged to have a front row seat to God's handiwork in our spouse's life, which allows us to see the good that God sees in them. This VIP seating provides the framework for perfect love.

**Prayer:** Lord, help us to be patient with one another's shortcomings and value your handiwork in our lives. Amen.

# DAY 198

*Each soul has an angel appointed to guard it from its birth.*

— *St. Jerome*

During morning prayers each day Kathleen asks the guardian angels of Troy and each of our children to protect them. This simple prayer brings incredible peace of mind. Knowing our spouse has an angel that was assigned to watch over and protect him or her from birth is a tremendous gift. When Troy travels for work, there are often periods of time when we are unable to connect due to time zones and busy schedules. Asking his guardian angel to protect his heart, mind, body, and soul has brought such peace of mind and comfort when anxiety is an issue. The angels are supernatural gifts from God to aid us in our spiritual life. We can pray daily for each family member to be protected by their guardian angel and call on our spouse's angel when we are concerned for their physical or spiritual safety.

**Prayer:** Angel of God, my guardian dear, to whom God's love commits me here, ever this day be at my side, to light, to guard, to rule, to guide. Amen. (Guardian Angel Prayer)

# DAY 199

*Let go of your plans. The first hour of your morning*
*belongs to God. Tackle the day's work that he charges you*
*with and he will give you the power to accomplish it.*

— *St. Teresa Benedicta of the Cross*

Many years ago, a wise priest told Kathleen, "If you do not give the first moment of your day to God, Satan is standing by ready to take it." These sensible words have been a driving force over the years. Before she even gets out of bed, Kathleen offers her day to God and asks him to help her to be faithful in her vocation as a wife and mother that day — to do his will, not her own. When we married, we began doing our own morning prayer of surrender together. We pray to protect our marriage from evil and to strengthen our relationship as one before God. Over the years, our morning prayer together has evolved to accommodate various seasons in our lives, but we strive to begin each day by connecting through prayer in some way, whether it is over the phone, in person, or simply praying for one another at the start of a new day.

**Prayer:** Lord, help us begin each day before your throne in a prayer of surrender to your will. May this daily prayer together be a source of many graces for our marriage. Amen.

# Day 200

*Great fruits are expected when the Divine*
*Law is kept by a devout soul.*

— *Pope St. Paul VI*

Marriage is rewarding when it is lived according to God's design. Don't sell yourself short! In his encyclical *Humanae Vitae*, Pope St. Paul VI presents us a roadmap to discover who we truly are before God and how we are created to relate, to love, and to be loved. It also boldly proclaims the dangers of a contraceptive mentality. Don't buy the lie! Contraception is not freedom; it enslaves us in our own passions and makes us incapable of giving ourselves freely and fully to each other in the marital act. When we contracept, we close off our marriage to God's creative love for us. We also withhold part of ourselves from each other. There is nothing to be afraid of! God has a beautiful plan for us and for our families — one that brings us deep joy. When it comes to the most intimate aspect of our marriage, it's important to remember that love is not authentic unless it is free, and perfect love casts out fear.

**Prayer:** Lord, we desire to experience marriage in all its fullness according to your plan. Please help us not to be afraid to embrace the fruitfulness of marital love. Amen.

# Day 201

*Brethren, I do not consider that I have made it my
own; but one thing I do, forgetting what lies behind
and straining forward to what lies ahead.*

— *Philippians 3:13*

One of the most life-giving actions in marriage is to wholeheartedly let go of past hurts that occurred because of something our spouse did or did not do. When a current circumstance in our marriage opens up a past wound, it may be tempting to remind our spouse of the pain they previously inflicted. But while we may want to revel in the feeling of justification for our own disordered response, holding onto the past discourages our spouse from doing what is right in the moment. It also keeps us from moving forward. If we give too much thought to the past or burden ourselves with concern for the future, we miss the joy of living in the present moment where God wants to work powerfully in our marriages.

**Prayer:** Lord, help us let go of past hurts that threaten to stifle the life out of our marriage. Teach us how to live in the present each moment, detached and healed from the pain of the past and full of hope for the future. Amen.

# Day 202

*I understood that every flower created by him is beautiful,*
*that the brilliance of the rose and the whiteness of*
*the lily do not lessen the perfume of the violet or the*
*sweet simplicity of the daisy. … If every tiny flower*
*wanted to be a rose, spring would lose its loveliness.*

— St. Thérèse of Lisieux

It does not matter whether we are a lily or a rose, a daisy, or a violet. What does matter is that we be who God calls us to be and we do it well. As married couples, we are on the same team but we each have different gifts, limitations, and life experiences we bring to the table. Our spouse is our partner, not our competition, and we are intended to collaborate in our efforts for the greater good of our team (our family). When we work together, we make the best of our gifts, time, and resources. And we minimize the impact of our limitations. We've learned to view our gifts, time, and resources as a shared pool from which we both draw for the good of our family. When we see what we each bring to our marriage as a collective whole, to be used for the good of the family and society, we more naturally embrace our roles as husband and wife and develop a fruitful rhythm in our marriage.

**Prayer:** Lord, may we use the gifts, resources, and time you have given us for the good of our marriage and family. Amen.

# Day 203

*Christ has no body now but yours. No hands, no feet*
*on earth, but yours. Yours are the eyes through which*
*Christ looks compassion into the world. Yours are*
*the feet with which Christ walks to do good. Yours*
*are the hands with which he blesses the world.*

— *Attributed to St. Teresa of Ávila*

Our bodies are chosen by God to be a living representation of Christ to our spouse. He chose Kathleen's feet to walk Troy to heaven. He chose Troy's hands to care for and bless Kathleen. And he chose our eyes to see each other's worth. This is our calling and our honor. Married love is the perfect mirror of Christ's love for the Church. We see a direct earthly image of how much Christ truly loves the Church when we witness the exchange of love between a husband and a wife in marriage. Spouses are called to be living icons reflecting Christ to one another, and together to the whole of society. This can only be accomplished when we freely walk in the will of God. Too many of us ask God to guide our footsteps when we're not willing to move our feet!

**Prayer:** Thank you, Lord, for your living presence in each of us. May we draw nearer to you as we draw closer to one another. Amen.

# DAY 204

*Every one then who hears these words of mine and does*
*them will be like a wise man who built his house upon*
*the rock; and the rain fell, and the floods came, and*
*the winds blew and beat upon that house, but it did*
*not fall, because it had been founded on the rock.*

— *Matthew 7:24–25*

A few weeks after we moved to South Carolina, contractors laid the foundation for a new home on the lot next door to us. We were amazed at how long the foundation took to complete. Once a solid foundation was built, however, the rest of the house went up very quickly. Marriage is like building a house. When we take the time to build a solid foundation on Christ, the ins and outs of each day run considerably more smoothly and function in proper order. Without God as our foundation, marriage is more likely to give way when the pressures of life become overbearing. Past experiences or a troubled upbringing may have made it difficult to know love the way God intends it to be lived and expressed. But it's never too late to learn how to love and to build a foundation on Christ. Find couples who model Christ's love; observe and learn from them. Then strive to emulate the way they live as three: husband and wife united in Christ.

**Prayer:** Lord, help us build a firm foundation on you, the source of our love and sacramental grace. Amen.

# Day 205

*The most deadly poison of our time is indifference.*

— *St. Maximilian Kolbe*

Indifference is a particularly deadly poison in marriage. When either spouse becomes apathetic, the marriage is in danger. Although arguments and power struggles are not ideal, they do indicate that each person is still engaged in the marriage and eager to fight for it. And our marriages are worth fighting for! While we cannot and should not hide our imperfections and human frailty from our spouse, it is good to consider that we are both imperfect individuals striving to perfect ourselves through the Sacrament of Matrimony. When difficulties arise and we are tempted to question the love we once felt for our spouse, we must intentionally choose to stay engaged in our marriage and pursue real love — the love that God designed and created for marriage alone!

**Prayer:** Lord, we ask you to help us always stay engaged in our marriage and keep us from growing indifferent. Amen.

# Day 206

*This is the day which the Lord has made;*
*let us rejoice and be glad in it.*

*— Psalm 118:24*

When we do not give the first moments of our day to God, the enemy is standing by ready to take them. Begin the day with a morning offering to consecrate all we do to Our Lord. We are always better off when we ask him to show us his plan for our day and then trust him for the grace to do it. The way we carry on throughout the day is a direct result of the way we start the day; our mindset and attitude set the tone. We often dress our opportunities and responsibilities as stress, but they are in fact blessings. Decide not to complain about the interruptions or setbacks you may have as you strive to accomplish the work entrusted to you each day. Rather, recognize the setbacks and interruptions as part of God's plan and make it a point to open each day with an "I-am-blessed-to" mentality instead of an "I-have-to" mentality.

**Prayer:** Lord, help us see each day as a gift. Help us to align our plans with yours, and give us the grace to do your will each day. Amen.

# Day 207

*Be still, and know that I am God.*

— *Psalm 46:10*

When we were first married, we made a decision to attend a Holy Hour together every week. For the first several years of our marriage, Tuesday was our night. From 9:00 to 10:00 p.m., we would spend time together alone with Our Lord in the Blessed Sacrament. Our "date night with Jesus" has evolved over the years as children have come along and business travel has intensified. But we have been showered with so many marital graces over the years that our couple Holy Hour has remained a top priority. Placing our Eucharistic Lord at the center of our marriage has given us the strength to love when it was difficult, the ability to forgive when our hearts were hardened, the courage to say "I am sorry" when pride would have led us to dig in, and the power to practice selflessness when selfishness was the more tempting road to take. Try spending time together with your spouse in adoration. We believe that you will see a qualitative difference in your marriage if you do.

**Prayer:** Lord, we thank you for your Eucharistic presence. May we never take for granted the gift of your body and blood truly present to us. Amen.

# Day 208

*Bear one another's burdens, and so fulfil the law of Christ.*

— *Galatians 6:2*

Our friend, Ginger, was sexually assaulted at twelve. This caused serious damage to her self-esteem and understanding of authentic love. Consequently, she spent years searching for love in all the wrong places and coming up empty. Eventually, Ginger married a man who was physically and mentally abusive. After three children and eight painful years, Ginger divorced her first husband. Unable to see God present in her life and feeling void of real love, she returned to her former patterns of self-destructive behavior.

When Ginger met Jeff, she was a broken, divorced mom of three and certain he would abandon her like so many other men in her life had previously done. But she soon realized he accepted her, baggage and all. Jeff didn't try to change her; rather, he loved her for who she was and where she was. Through Jeff's unconditional love, Ginger came to experience and know the love of God. Jeff and Ginger have now been married for twelve beautiful years. Jeff's willingness to "bear" Ginger's "burdens" and love her despite her past opened her up to a love she never knew possible.

**Prayer:** Lord, please give us the strength and courage to bear one another's burdens with love. Amen.

# Day 209

*Would to God that his well-beloved son was invited to every
marriage, as he was to the marriage at Cana, for then the wine
of his consolation and blessing would never be lacking to it.*

— *St. Francis de Sales*

Let's face it. Every marriage has its tough moments. Reflect no further
than the most recent squabble in your own marriage. Conflict is as
inevitable as death and taxes. However, how we together *deal* with conflict determines whether we're kissing and making up, or building a wall
between us. Fortunately, St. Francis de Sales gives us a roadmap here: "If
only Jesus were invited to every marriage . . ." St. Francis de Sales chooses
Jesus' first miracle of turning water into wine as the symbol for the wellspring of love between spouses whenever Jesus is present. It is important
for us to remember that just as the water vessels were completely empty
before Jesus' arrival on the scene, so too is the heart and soul of marriage
when it is devoid of Christ.

**Prayer:** Lord, may our marriage never be void of you. We invite you into
every area of our lives. Fill us with your love. Amen.

# DAY 210

*Money we have not, but from our faith*
*will spring forth miracles.*

*— St. Frances Xavier Cabrini*

Some dear friends of ours have been full-time ministers during their entire marriage of eighteen years, while raising seven remarkable, faith-filled children. Money has always been tight for them, and they have often had to rely on the charity of others to make ends meet. A minister's salary is small, but the opportunities to witness God's providence are many! The stories this family has shared with us of how God has provided for each of their specific needs, often down to the dollar, are astounding. The financial sacrifices they have made to say yes to God's calling and mission for their marriage and family might have caused some to lose their faith or take a different path. And yet, this family never doubts that God will give them what they need, when they need it, and how they need it. From their deep faith and trust in God has literally sprung forth miracles that have not only blessed their family but have been a witness to the power of believing in and relying on God's divine provision.

**Prayer:** Lord, help us to always trust in your provision for all our needs, and show us how we can support others who need our help to follow your will in their lives. Amen.

# Day 211

*Enter by the narrow gate; for the gate is wide*
*and the way is easy, that leads to destruction,*
*and those who enter by it are many.*

— *Matthew 7:13*

Most people do not purposely choose hell. In and of itself, evil is not appealing. Satan knows this, so when the inevitable stresses of day-to-day married life become taxing, the devil is ready to provide us "relief" through an alternative path which falsely promises to give us everything we want. The problem with this tempting option is that it literally leads to a dead end. As married couples, we must put holy hedges around our marriages to safeguard them. If we find ourselves on the wrong path, we must own it and get the help needed to save our marriages and preserve our souls. We want to follow the path to heaven together with our spouse. It is much narrower than the path to hell, but it is the path that will bring us authentic joy.

**Prayer:** Lord, thank you for the gift of eternal life. Help us to live our vocation of marriage on the path that take us ultimately to heaven. Amen.

# DAY 212

*When God Yahweh said, "It is not good that man*
*should be alone" (Gn 2:18), he affirmed that "alone"*
*man does not completely realize this essence. He realizes*
*it only by existing "with someone" and even more*
*deeply and completely — by existing "for someone."*

— *Pope St. John Paul II*

It was Father's Day, and Kathleen was sitting at the Philadelphia International Airport waiting for a shuttle bus to take her to a week-long immersion course on St. John Paul II's Theology of the Body. Troy had attended the same workshop the year before and insisted that Kathleen follow suit. But Kathleen felt terrible leaving him on such a special day that honors his vocation as father to our five beautiful children. She will never forget his response: "Honey, the fruit that will come from both of us having this experience is the greatest gift we can give our marriage and our children." And it has been. We all long to be seen and known for who we are. It is the way God created us. A deeper study of the Theology of the Body taught the two of us how to truly see one another with God's eyes. It took our marriage to the next level of intimacy, for which we are both grateful.

**Prayer:** Lord, help us to see one another as you see us and to truly know one another through your eyes. Amen.

# Day 213

*What peace floods a soul when it soars above natural feelings!*
*The joy of the truly poor in spirit is beyond compare.*

— *St. Thérèse of Lisieux*

We must never let our feelings control us. But being in control of our feelings can be extremely difficult. Have you ever said something in anger that you later regretted? We have. That's because emotions are powerful, and they can often determine how spouses interact. We are called to "soar above natural feelings," but this is an acquired skill that requires practice and dedication. Governing our emotions, however, does not mean suppressing them. In fact, suppressing our feelings can lead us to unhealthy coping practices. It is important to acknowledge how we feel, but also understand that our emotions should not control us. From time to time, it's good to consider the emotional lenses through which we are viewing our marriage. Perhaps we need to reframe our thoughts to create a more realistic view that brings our reason and emotions together.

**Prayer:** Lord, teach us how to control our emotions and reframe our thoughts toward one another when necessary. Amen.

# Day 214

*Preach the gospel always and if necessary, use words.*

— *Attributed to St. Francis of Assisi*

One fall evening a few years ago, our oldest daughter captured a short video on her phone of the two of us spontaneously dancing together in our foyer after dinner. The little kids were running circles around us, and Kathleen's shirt was soaking wet from cleaning dishes. Yet in that moment, we spun around to "Dancing Queen" without a care in the world. Our eyes were fixed on one another, and the love we shared conveyed to our children the beauty of marriage. A good marriage is made up of thousands of these ordinary moments — not just a handful of occasions staged a few days a year, but every day. Love grows and blossoms in the nitty-gritty trenches of the domestic church. That is where we preach the gospel of marriage according to God's plan without words.

**Prayer:** Lord, help us to "preach the gospel" in our marriage daily, with both words and actions. Amen.

# DAY 215

*What does matter is that we engrave, that we burn upon
our souls the conviction that Christ's invitation to sanctity,
which he addresses to all men without exception, puts each
one of us under an obligation to cultivate our interior life
and to struggle daily to practice the Christian virtues.*

— *St. Josemaría Escrivá*

The sanctity of marriage is threatened. Divorce rates are alarmingly high, same-sex unions have not just been legalized but affirmed on a global scale, and cohabiting before marriage or without marital commitment has become the norm. How much more, then, should we strive to live our vocation of marriage with integrity, passion, and purpose? Christ invites us to become saints through faithfully living the Sacrament of Matrimony. When a marriage glorifies God, it upholds the sanctity of the sacrament. Husbands and wives have a responsibility to cultivate a virtuous life together and become the evangelizers of other marriages through the power of their example. A healthy and holy marriage is a living, breathing, and active signpost, pointing people in the direction of God's love. A marriage visibly lived according to God's plan is an invitation to others to discover God's plan for them.

**Prayer:** Lord, we accept your invitation to become saints. Help us live lives of holiness and become a living example of your plan for marriage. Amen.

# DAY 216

*From silly devotions and sour-faced saints, Lord, deliver us!*

*— Attributed to St. Teresa of Ávila*

We had a very heated conversation early on in our marriage. Kathleen was yelling some very hurtful words at Troy but then had the sudden realization that she was pushing him further away from herself and from God by her sinful behavior. Her intention to draw him closer to her heart and to God's plan for our marriage completely backfired. But becoming aware of that helped both of us to move in a much more positive direction. Do we attract people when we convey our love for God, or do we repel them? Does the way we live our faith draw our spouse closer to us or push them away? If we hope to encourage our spouse in their walk with God, then it is imperative that the way we live as husband or wife is appealing. If we claim to love God, but go about our day complaining or neglecting responsibilities to devote more time to religious activities, our spouse isn't likely to think much of our faith.

**Prayer:** Lord, may our love for you be the driving force in our love for one another. Deliver us from presenting that love in an unattractive way. Amen.

# DAY 217

*God has created me to do him some definite*
*service. He has committed some work to me*
*which he has not committed to another.*

— *St. John Henry Newman*

How is God calling us to serve him in our vocation of marriage? What unique service has he entrusted to us as a couple? Do we know? Do we ask God to show us? God has a specific plan and purpose not just for marriage in general, but for our marriage specifically. He brought us together with each of our unique gifts, limitations, and life experiences to fulfill the mission he has entrusted to us. It is up to each couple to seek and discover God's calling for their marriage. That involves relinquishing control and trusting him to fulfill his mission of love in us. God's plan is ongoing; it's not one and done. This means that marriage is to be lived in a constant state of openness to the will of God, so he can continually work in and through us as a couple.

**Prayer:** Lord, help us to live our marriage in a state of perpetual openness to your will. Work in and through us to fulfill the mission you have entrusted to our care. Amen.

# DAY 218

*Courage! Do not fall back.*

— *St. Joan of Arc*

Simple, short words of wisdom from a saint who led armies to victory through her faith in God. How easy it is to get discouraged when trouble comes our way or things are not going as we had hoped or planned. What is needed is courage!

- Courage to love when it is difficult to love
- Courage to get up when we are knocked down
- Courage to apologize with sincerity
- Courage to forgive despite the lack of a sincere apology
- Courage to die to ourselves so our marriage can thrive
- Courage to sacrifice for our beloved even when they don't deserve it
- Courage to keep moving forward when we want to give up

Do we want to have a healthy, holy, and dynamic marriage? Then we must embrace the virtue of courage in all things.

**Prayer:** Lord, grow our faith so we may live our marriage boldly and courageously in alignment with your will. Amen.

# Day 219

*The steadfast love of the LORD never ceases,*
*his mercies never come to an end.*

— *Lamentations 3:22*

Human love is imperfect. Spouses, children, friends, and family will disappoint us from time to time — perhaps even fail us. But God's love is perfect. We have each experienced the most significant spiritual growth during the most difficult seasons in our marriage. Then, we rightly looked to God to fulfill us instead of our spouse. When he is all we have, our friendship with him blossoms in amazing and beautiful ways. When a spouse does not reciprocate the love we give, we may be tempted to look outside the marriage to fulfill that very real need. What often begins as innocent curiosity can lead to a full-blown emotional attachment and even sexual infidelity before we know it. The slippery slope is just that — slippery! Just know that even when we're struggling, we can rely on God's love completely and trust that his love alone will suffice. It is better to be alone with God than to jeopardize our marriage and our soul by looking for love elsewhere.

**Prayer:** Lord, your love alone is perfect. May we always rely on your love and accept the fact that in our human nature, we will fail one another from time to time. Amen.

# Day 220

*Do not put off to tomorrow, the good you can do today.*

— *St. John Bosco*

There is no promise of tomorrow, so we must love our spouse today! This means telling them how much we love them and why. Kissing them good morning and hugging them goodnight. Praying with them. Listening to them. Opening our heart to them. Expressing appreciation for all they do. Picking up the dirty socks from the floor. Resisting spending money we don't really have. Cuddling and then consummating our marriage. Cooking a nice dinner. Eating a meal together. Turning the television off and putting the cell phones down. Playing a game or going for a walk. The opportunities we have today could be gone tomorrow.

**Prayer:** Lord, help us to invest in our marriage every day and never put off what we can do today to help our marriage grow. Amen.

# DAY 221

*Bad times, hard times, this is what people keep saying;*
*but let us live well, and times shall be good. We are*
*the times: Such as we are, such are the times.*

— *St. Augustine of Hippo*

We have all been pursued at one time or another by an insurance company via snail mail, email, phone call, or a personal visit. Each company competes for our business, and we have to choose the right policy to fit our specific needs, circumstances, and budget. Why do we need insurance? Even when it is not specifically required, we often choose to invest in policies that can protect us from circumstances that could literally wipe us out financially. Insurance gives us peace of mind. So, how can we protect our marriage from devastating circumstances? By living our marriage well. Marriage is an investment, one of the richest investments we will ever make. How much of ourselves we invest in marriage will determine how our "times" together will be.

**Prayer:** Lord, give us the grace to change our "times" by allowing your grace to change us. Amen.

# Day 222

*Love ought to manifest itself in deeds rather than words.*

— *St. Ignatius of Loyola*

We decided early on in our marriage that we would have a date night once a week. But soon, once a week turned into once a month, and once a month slipped into every other month. Something else always seemed to take priority. In the book *By Love Refined: Letters to a Young Bride,* Alice Von Hildebrand recalls the Gospel story of the Transfiguration and talks about the importance of having a "Tabor Vision" of your spouse. When we fall in love, we are granted a perception of our beloved's true self, who they are genuinely meant to be at the deepest level. While others see primarily our spouse's exterior acts, and in particular their failings, we are given the honor of seeing the beauty of our beloved. We are called to keep alive the flame of love that once overwhelmed us. It may not always be possible to go out, but date nights and opportunities to spend time alone together are essential to a thriving and successful marriage.

**Prayer:** Lord, thank you for the Tabor Vision you gave us of one another. Help us to keep it at the forefront of our minds every day. Amen.

# Day 223

*Little children, let us not love in word or*
*speech but in deed and in truth.*

— *1 John 3:18*

The way we treat our spouse profoundly influences both their self-worth and the way they see God. We all have an internal radar that detects whether our spouse's love is real or self-serving. Real love is not about feelings, but it is about who we are and how we love when the feelings fade. Love is a daily decision but should never be viewed as a duty. True love encourages. We are our spouse's advocate, and our belief in who they are pushes them onward in Christ. The greatest joy in marriage, one that should far outweigh any success or achievement, is to see our spouse displaying godly attributes. The highest purpose of marital love is fulfilled when we lead one another to be more Christlike.

**Prayer:** Lord, give us eyes to see our spouse's value, and a voice to encourage them to seek you and do your will. Amen.

# DAY 224

*For he satisfies him who is thirsty,*
*and the hungry he fills with good things.*

— *Psalms 107:9*

There are countless people, circumstances, and experiences that will bring us happiness and pleasure, but only God can satisfy the deepest longing of our hearts. His joy is eternal, and the joys of this world — including our marriage and family — are temporal. This does not mean that we should not enjoy God's gifts and blessings. But it is important to recognize that the things of this life were never meant to fill the void that only God can fill. As much as we love our husband or wife and enjoy his or her company, our spouse will never fully satisfy the hunger in our heart that can be satisfied by God alone.

**Prayer:** Lord, keep us from placing unrealistic expectations on one another. Teach us to look to you to fulfill all our needs. Amen.

# Day 225

*Death and life are in the power of the tongue,*
*and those who love it will eat its fruits.*

*— Proverbs 18:21*

There is no erase button when it comes to the words we say. Once they leave our lips, we cannot retract them. Words can build up, bless, encourage and motivate, or they can tear down, hurt, and cause lasting scars. We should be careful to choose our words wisely when speaking to our spouse. We have seen the damage to our marriage that unkind words blurted out in the heat of the moment have caused. Saying something mean only creates more problems, while speaking love heals and grows our marriage. Our words to each other must breathe life and point us to God. His voice is the voice we want our spouse to hear through us, even when we have to communicate difficult truths.

**Prayer:** Breathe on me, breath of God, and let my words breathe life into my marriage. Amen.

# DAY 226

*Worry is a weakness from which very few of us are entirely free. We must be on guard against this most insidious enemy of our peace of soul. Instead, let us foster confidence in God and thank him ahead of time for whatever he chooses to send us.*

— *Bl. Solanus Casey*

Throughout his twenties, most of Troy's free time was spent sailing. One life lesson he took away from his sailing years is that we cannot control the wind, but we can adjust the sail. In fact, his final test to become a skipper was taken on Lake Minnetonka in Minnesota, right as a storm was brewing. It was Troy's job to work with the wind and not against it by adjusting and readjusting the sails in order to bring the ship safely back to shore. Marriage requires the learned skill of being flexible and working with what we have to make the most of a given situation. Often, we cannot change a circumstance, but we can adjust our attitude — our "sails" — to work with it. Worry is natural, but it moves us nowhere. Instead, we can trust in God's provision and take control of the sails to carefully lead our marriage through turbulent storms.

**Prayer:** Lord, please be the captain of our ship and lead us securely through the things we cannot control. Amen.

# Day 227

*God is faithful, and he will not let you be tempted beyond
your strength, but with the temptation will also provide
the way of escape, that you may be able to endure it.*

*— 1 Corinthians 10:13*

Marriage matters because it is God's path to holiness. Guided and strengthened by the grace of God, husband and wife "advance their own perfection, as well as their mutual sanctification, and hence contribute jointly to the glory of God" (*Gaudium et Spes*, 48). Daily yeses to the will of God and striving to continually open ourselves up to renewal and transformation by the Holy Spirit is what being faithful looks like.

Will you fail? Yes.

Will you struggle? Yes.

Will you argue? Yes.

But keep trying. Keep giving yourself to love's costly sacrifice of self — one day, one struggle, one laugh, one divine moment at a time. Share the parts of yourself that you would rather hide. Be consistent and dedicated to learning about one another, serving one another, encouraging one another, and forgiving one another. This is your calling.

**Prayer:** Lord, strengthened and guided by your grace, may we advance in holiness each day through our mutual love for one another and our commitment to your calling. Amen.

# DAY 228

*Do not be deceived: "Bad company ruins good morals."*

— *1 Corinthians 15:33*

We are the sum of the people we spend the most time with. If we surround ourselves with people who are striving to live lives of holiness, especially other married couples, then we will be inspired and encouraged in our own vocation. Likewise, if we hang out with married men and women who disrespect their spouse and disregard the sanctity of their marriage, then we likely will be discouraged and demotivated to uphold the dignity of our own. What we love and who we spend our time with will shape who we become and affect what we have to offer our spouse and family.

**Prayer:** Lord, show us not only how to love, but what and whom to love. Please surround us with married couples who love their vocation and who are striving to live it according to you will. Amen.

# DAY 229

*Finally, be strong in the Lord and in the strength of*
*his might. Put on the whole armor of God, that you*
*may be able to stand against the wiles of the devil.*

*— Ephesians 6:10–11*

This is a sure way to prove our love for our spouse. Fighting the good fight to nourish and protect our soul and steering clear of sinful situations and dangerous pits shouts "I love you!" and "I love our marriage!" We are surrounded by temptations of every kind, and apart from consistent daily prayer and frequent confession, we will fall into sin. We must put hedges around our marriage and safety locks on our love to safeguard our sacramental life together. Don't spend too much time with that friend who disregards our values; don't watch that raunchy television show that plants negative and impure thoughts in our head; don't go to that happy hour after work instead of spending time with our family. Each choice we make has the power to strengthen the dignity of your marriage or weaken the link of our love.

**Prayer:** Lord, please give us the strength each day to do what is right for our marriage and help us resist temptations that present themselves in our lives. Amen.

# Day 230

*Remember this and never forget it: even if it should
seem at times that everything is collapsing, nothing is
collapsing at all, because God does not lose battles.*

— *St. Josemaría Escrivá*

God is always on the winning team! In his book *Winning Every Day,*
legendary Notre Dame football coach Lou Holtz used the simple
but powerful acronym W.I.N. to explain the process of winning. It is doing "What's Important Now." He instructed his players to ask themselves
this question thirty-five times a day: "What is important right now, in
this moment?" Then do it. If you want to "win" at marriage, then do the
next right thing, and then the next. The only person we can control is
ourselves — not our spouse, not our family, not our employer. We can
influence others, but we can only manage our own behaviors. When it
seems as if everything around us is collapsing, do the next right thing,
give it to God and trust that we are on the winning team.

**Prayer:** Lord, help us to trust that you will use all things for our good,
and remind us that we are on your winning team. Amen.

# Day 231

*People hate the truth for the sake of whatever it is they love more than the truth. They love truth when it shines warmly on them and hate it when it rebukes them.*

*— St. Augustine of Hippo*

Throughout the first few years of our marriage, Troy relished the freedom that came from taking periodic business trips. He admits that he enjoyed not having to be accountable to Kathleen. Troy didn't feel the need to tell her how he spent his time, nor did he want to feel micromanaged from afar. He thought being a good husband and dad when he was home was enough. So, he justified bad behavior while he was away on business because he loved his freedom more than he loved the truth of the pain and mistrust he had created. Troy wasn't necessarily doing anything sinful during his free time, but he didn't like feeling bound by the responsibility to stay emotionally connected. Eventually, we figured out how to keep our marriage strong when travel pulled us apart. Although this was one of the most painful seasons of our marriage, God stretched us, and we grew in amazing ways as a couple because of our willingness to make the necessary changes and cooperate with his grace.

**Prayer:** Lord, help us to seek, love, and live truth in our marriage. Amen.

# Day 232

*Pay attention carefully. After the sin comes the shame;*
*courage follows repentance. Did you pay attention*
*to what I said? Satan upsets the order; he gives*
*courage to sin and the shame to repentance.*

— *St. John Chrysostom*

There are two types of sins: sins of commission and sins of omission. Sins of commission are those sinful actions that we choose to do. Sins of omission occur when we fail to do something that is right. Sins of commission are often easily recognizable in marriage, while sins of omission can sometimes be more difficult to detect. If a spouse says something hurtful, they can be called out on it. But if they withhold important information, we might not even be aware of the sin until the effects of it are manifested in our marriage. When we sin, the effects of it are felt most often and most deeply by those with whom we are closest. In marriage, when one spouse sins, the other spouse suffers the effect of that sin right along with their beloved because the two have become one. Three of the most powerful words that can be uttered in any relationship, and especially in marriage, are "I am sorry." Apologizing with sincerity and authentic regret gives meaning and weight to the words themselves and brings healing.

**Prayer:** Lord, may we have the humility to admit when we are wrong and apologize sincerely to our spouse when necessary. Amen.

# Day 233

*God dwells in the inmost depths of the soul, and therefore*
*there is nothing within that is hidden from him.*

— *St. Teresa Benedicta of the Cross*

One year after we moved in, we discovered our house had a termite problem. Our son Joseph was three years old at the time. He was playing in our covered porch, when he suddenly witnessed thousands of termites emerge from a hole in the wood near the bottom of a window frame. He ran inside and exclaimed, "Bugs, bugs, lots of bugs!" Through that experience we learned that termites thrive in dark and damp areas, but when they are exposed to the light, they die within minutes. It is the same with sin. When we expose our sins before God, our eternal Light, they can no longer thrive. There is nothing we can hide from God, but we have free will, and bringing our sins to the light of his grace and mercy is a choice. Sadly, many people not only try to conceal their sinful tendencies from God, but from their spouse as well. Freedom comes in exposing our sins to the grace of God's healing power and allowing our spouse to be a part of that journey.

**Prayer:** Lord, help us always bring our sins to the light of your grace and mercy through the gift of the Sacrament of Reconciliation. Amen.

# Day 234

*It is better to illuminate than to shine.*

— *St. Thomas Aquinas*

By divine design, Our Lord gave men and woman different gifts and abilities to help them fulfill complementary roles as husband and wife. We are hardwired by God to complement our spouse in our marriage through our unique feminine and masculine qualities. At a given time, one of us may shine through a particular gift, but overall, it is best to allow our talents and abilities to continually illuminate our marriage, rather than trying to take center stage. If a husband or wife feels incompetent in comparison to the other, this can lead to low self-esteem and a lack of motivation to contribute their gifts to the marriage. Complementarity calls us to unite our efforts as husband and wife in such a way that we enhance and illuminate the attributes each of us has.

**Prayer:** Lord, help us complement one another as husband and wife through the unique gifts and talents you have given us. May your blessings inspire us to illuminate one another. Amen.

# DAY 235

*A man would do nothing if he waited until he could*
*do it so well that no one could find fault.*

— *St. John Henry Newman*

When a husband or wife feels defeated, they quickly lose motivation to make any attempt to please their spouse moving forward. Understanding what makes one another come alive and what causes the other to emotionally retreat requires our attention throughout our marriage. Sometimes, it is much easier to identify our spouse's faults than it is to recognize their gifts and good behaviors. We must be on the lookout for good things rather than faults, and when we see them, we must be quick to acknowledge them. Every husband and wife should be able to find the admiration and respect they crave from their spouse. We are to be one another's greatest cheerleader. Consider it an honor.

**Prayer:** Lord, help us continually see the good in one another and build each other up, rather than tear one another down. Amen.

# Day 236

*The Lord gave, and the Lord has taken*
*away; blessed be the name of the Lord.*

— *Job 1:21*

We all have an ego. Whether we're men pushing for a work promotion or to win the next recreational basketball game, or women flaunting our God-given gifts for worldly persuasion, we all tend toward some form of selfishness. Likewise, we all go through adversity in one way or another. We must be cautious not to allow ourselves to be taken down by adversity, nor to give into vanity during times of prosperity. As husbands and wives, we must recognize that all prosperity and blessings come from God. But God also allows adversity into our lives to strengthen our faith and our love for one another.

**Prayer:** Lord, just like Job, may we honor and love you and one another regardless of whether we are in a season of prosperity or adversity. Amen.

# DAY 237

*Things were in God's plan which I had not planned*
*at all. I am coming to the living faith and conviction*
*that — from God's point of view — there is no chance*
*and that the whole of my life, down to every detail, has*
*been mapped out in God's divine providence and makes*
*complete and perfect sense in God's all-seeing eyes.*

— *St. Teresa Benedicta of the Cross*

When Kathleen was a student, she met with Fr. Michael Scanlan, the former president of Franciscan University of Steubenville, to ask him how to follow God's plan each day. He shared that he went to the chapel each morning and presented his plan for the day to God. Fr. Scanlan would literally open his Franklin Planner in the chapel and pray, "This is my plan today, is it in line with your will? What do I need to tweak or change?" The plan we initially envisioned for our lives and marriage has looked quite different as it has unfolded over the years. Although there was much in "our plans" that was not part of God's plan at all, we can clearly see in retrospect just how perfect God's plan truly is — down to every detail.

**Prayer:** Lord, we know that your blueprint for our marriage is far more than we can imagine, and that is exciting! Help us surrender to your will one day at a time. Amen.

# DAY 238

*Nothing is so strong as gentleness; nothing
is so gentle as real strength.*

— *St. Francis de Sales*

With all of our children's grandparents deceased, we prayed for a couple that would take our children on and love them as their own grandchildren. In his time, God eventually blessed our five children with a faithful and loving couple from our church who have been an incredible gift to our family. Pete is a retired Chicago policeman and a Vietnam veteran. He is firm in his convictions, a protector at heart, and yet as gentle and loving as they come. He demands respect, but in the most tender and loving way. Men, this is the kind of man God is calling us to be — gentle at heart, yet full of strength and conviction. Our wives and children need to feel protected and secure under the umbrella of our love. They need to know that we will fight for them and protect them not only physically, but also emotionally and spiritually.

**Prayer:** Lord, help me be the man you are calling me to be for my family, a protector full of strength and conviction, but one who is gentle. Amen.

# Day 239

*Beneath the cross one learns to love.*

— *St. Pio of Pietrelcina*

There is a beautiful Croatian wedding tradition. The priest blesses a crucifix, then the bride places her right hand on the crucifix and the groom places his hand over hers. The priest covers their hands with his stole as the bride and groom profess their vows. Each of them kiss the crucifix, the source of their love. It is assumed that if either the husband or wife abandon the other, they have let go of the cross. And if they have let go of the cross, they have let go of Christ. After the ceremony the newlyweds are encouraged to place their crucifix in a prominent place in their home as a reminder of the vows they made on their wedding day and the value of, and need for, sacrifice to faithfully live their marriage vows. Although neither of us is Croatian, we incorporated this tradition into our wedding ceremony. Our crucifix now hangs above our bed as a reminder to die to ourselves and learn love beneath the cross.

**Prayer:** Lord, may we continually cling to the cross, the source of your love and our salvation. Amen.

# Day 240

*You will seek me and find me; when you
seek me with all your heart.*

— *Jeremiah 29:13*

God persistently pursues us and longs for us to grow in our knowledge of him and deepen our love for him. Likewise, we are called to relentlessly pursue our spouse in love and strive to grow in our knowledge of who he or she is. The love we have for our husband or wife is meant to mirror the love God has for us. We must never stop seeking our beloved. The beginning of married life is not the end of the quest. On the contrary, it is the beginning. Our spouse is a gift, a mystery that requires continual discovery throughout our journey together.

**Prayer:** Lord, may we continually discover the treasures we each have to offer, and may our discoveries draw us into closer union with you. Amen.

# Day 241

*Love is a mystery that transforms everything*
*it touches into things beautiful and pleasing to*
*God. The love of God makes a soul free.*

— *St. Faustina Maria Kowalska*

How can love transform your marriage? What needs does your husband or wife have that you can realistically meet? Instead of playing mind games or sulking over the fact that your spouse is not treating you the way you want them to, let love turn your attention to their needs. Invest time in asking questions and observing what you can do to please your spouse. Is he hungering for sexual intimacy or craving time and attentiveness? Is she desperate for affirmation or tired and in need of rest? When Troy notices that Kathleen is worn out, he will often say, "What can I do to help?" This phrase is like gold to Kathleen. It says "I love you enough to notice." Even if there is nothing Troy can do in the moment, the fact that he recognizes the need fills Kathleen with love and rejuvenates her heart.

**Prayer:** Lord, help us recognize each other's needs and strive to meet these needs with your love. Amen.

# Day 242

*For to everyone who has will more be given, and*
*he will have abundance; but from him who has*
*not, even what he has will be taken away.*

— *Matthew 25:29*

We often forget that everything we have already belongs to God. Our money and possessions belong to him, and the talents he has blessed us with are to be used for his glory, not our own. When we place God first in our marriage, tithing comes naturally because we recognize that what we have been given is meant to be shared. The Church never asks us to give more than we can afford, but the reality is many can afford more than they actually give. We are encouraged to give a total of ten percent of our income off the top, our first fruits, as a donation which can be split between our local parish and other charitable organizations. We are further encouraged to give ten percent of our time to volunteering for worthy causes, and to use the talents God has given us to glorify him. God is never outdone in generosity. We always get back so much more than we give.

**Prayer:** Lord, we recognize that all we have is a gift from you. Give us the courage to be generous with our time, talents, and resources. Amen.

# Day 243

*Lord, make me an instrument of your peace. Where there is
hatred, let me sow love; where there is injury, pardon; where
there is doubt, faith; where there is despair, hope; where
there is darkness, light; and where there is sadness, joy.*

*— From the Prayer of St. Francis of Assisi*

Our mission in marriage is to be a channel of God's mercy and grace to our spouse and help one another get to heaven. The day-to-day demands and pressures of married life, however, can often give way to obstructing that channel and preventing the grace of God from freely flowing. What's the remedy?

When we feel hatred or disgust toward our spouse, sow love.

When we are wounded by our spouse's words or actions, practice pardon.

When we begin to doubt if our marriage is worth fighting for, have faith in God's plan.

When despair creeps in, push it out with hope.

When darkness takes over, be the light in our marriage.

When sadness tries to rob us, recall all that we have to be joyful for in our spouse.

**Prayer:** Lord, make us instruments of your peace. Amen.

# DAY 244

*O Divine master grant that I may not so much seek*
*to be consoled as to console, to be understood as to*
*understand; to be loved as to love. For it is in giving*
*that we receive, it is in pardoning that we are pardoned,*
*and it is in dying that we are born to eternal life.*

*— From the Prayer of St. Francis of Assisi*

Most couples start out doing all they can to love and serve their spouse, but somewhere along the journey, their willingness to jump through hoops for the other is replaced by a reluctance to even cross the room to do something for them. It is much easier to think of our own wants and needs than it is to focus on the wants and needs of our spouse — especially when our own needs aren't being met. When we are not aware of this tendency, selfishness can subtly begin to permeate a marriage. Unfortunately, we all have the selfish gene. But two people attempting to get their own way will never experience the oneness marriage is designed to foster. Marriage requires the gift of self — the gift of selflessness. And this gift is one that the sacramental grace of marriage empowers us to make.

**Prayer:** Lord, give us the grace we need to conquer our selfish nature, so we can make a sincere gift of ourselves to one another. Amen.

# Day 245

*All of the darkness in the world cannot
extinguish the light of a single candle.*

— *St. Francis of Assisi*

On the first anniversary of our son Dominic's death, our parish priest celebrated a special Mass in honor of his life. It was followed by a gathering with close family and friends in the church basement. We had set up a table to display a few mementos from Dominic's short life, including a special candle a close priest-friend had given us to light in Dominic's honor on special occasions. The celebration began around 8:00 p.m. The sun had set, and a storm was brewing. Suddenly, the electricity went out. The only light in the room full of people was the single candle lit in Dominic's honor on the table of mementos. That single candle lit up the room. We often think of this moment and the power of a single flame burning bright. When we go through the dark and difficult moments of marriage, it's comforting to know that one person shining bright with the love of Christ can change the entire dynamic. Every one of us can choose to be that light.

**Prayer:** Lord, may we always be your light to one another. Amen.

# Day 246

*That is why you go to pray: to become a bonfire,*
*a living flame giving light and heat.*

— *St. Josemaría Escrivá*

We both look forward to doing a holy hour of prayer each week. It fuels us to live each day for God. Spending time in front of Jesus present in the Blessed Sacrament is like soaking up the rays of God's graces and love. The more time spent there in prayer, the more on fire we will be. The graces we receive from our Eucharistic Lord pour over into our marriage and family as God intends. Our weekly holy hour further ignites the flame of God's love that already lives in our hearts. Be sure to devote quality time to God on a consistent basis so you can be a channel of God's grace to your spouse and family. Find the closest adoration chapel and schedule a date with Jesus!

**Prayer:** Lord, thank you for the gift of the Eucharist and for the spiritual benefits that come from spending time in your presence. Amen.

# DAY 247

*What use is it telling me that so and so is a good son of mine*
*— a good Christian — but a bad shoemaker? If he doesn't*
*try to learn his trade well, or doesn't give his full attention*
*to it, he won't be able to sanctify it or offer it to Our Lord.*

— *St. Josemaría Escrivá*

Sanctity consists in being faithful to our duties in life. We can pray two hours a day, volunteer several hours a week, go to daily Mass and stay for the Rosary, but if we are not responsibly and lovingly fulfilling what is required of us in our vocation of marriage, our virtuous actions are in vain. The fulcrum of true spirituality is found through the sanctification of the ordinary moments each day. When we care for the physical, emotional, and spiritual needs of our family, we are being faithful to the life God has entrusted to us. Each duty done in a spirit of love, driven by the grace of God, advances us on our spiritual journey. It may be less glamorous and pleasurable to take out the garbage, counsel a child, or listen to our spouse than it is to lead the church Bible study. But we must be faithful to God in what he has asked of us.

**Prayer:** Lord, thank you for the gift of our vocation of marriage. Help us to be faithful to our duties as husband and wife each day. Amen.

# DAY 248

*Don't say: "That person gets on my nerves."*
*Think: "That person sanctifies me."*

— *St. Josemaría Escrivá*

Marriage is a journey of two imperfect people striving to live lives of virtue through the ordinary moments each day with heaven as their ultimate goal. Our spouse and marriage will never be perfect, but there will be a lot of perfect moments that push us forward in love and keep us moving in the direction of heaven. When lived according to divine design, sacramental marriage is a path to sanctity. In the imperfect moments that annoy or frustrate us, we can redirect our thoughts to three things we love about our spouse. What are the last three house projects they willingly did? What are the last three tender moments of love we shared? What are the last three sacrifices they made? Shifting the focus from what gets on our nerves to what we are grateful for in our spouse perfects us and our marriage little by little.

**Prayer:** Lord, thank you for the gift of each other. May we grow together in holiness one day at a time. Help us to see what annoys us as your sanctifying work in our hearts. Amen.

# DAY 249

*I will bless the LORD at all times;*
*his praise shall continually be in my mouth.*

*— Psalm 34:1*

Our daughter Gemma attended a weekly Bible study for several years under the direction of Jess, a young college student at the time. Both Jess and her mom struggled with serious health issues, which required frequent medical intervention. Despite the burden she carried, Jess was always joyful, full of praise for God, and quick to ask others what she could pray for. Joy is a fruit of the Holy Spirit and a virtue, not a feeling. When put into action, it is attractive and has the ability to draw our spouse closer to our heart. A joyful heart is contagious and can bring light to a dismal situation, because joy is a sign of hope. So, whether we feel joyful or not, we can, and should, always choose joy as a way to grow in love as a married couple.

**Prayer:** Lord, we pray for the grace of joy, especially when our commitment to one another feels burdensome. Amen.

# DAY 250

*Hatred is not a creative force. Love alone*
*creates. Suffering will not prevail over us; it will*
*only melt us down and strengthen us.*

— *St. Maximilian Kolbe*

We don't live marriage in a bubble, so it can be tempting to place blame on external factors rather than take ownership of our own actions when troubles surface. It is easy to say that if only the kitchen sink didn't start leaking or the car didn't break down, we would not be fighting right now about how to manage our finances. This is life. External pressures are inevitable and will never go away. We must learn how to manage them in a healthy way that strengthens our marriage instead of weakening it. Blame will never solve a problem; love alone is a "creative force."

**Prayer:** Lord, may your love be the creative force in our marriage that propels us forward toward eternity with you. Amen.

# DAY 251

*Let your compassion come to me, that I may live;*
*for your law is my delight.*

— *Psalm 119:77*

When we love someone deeply, compassion comes naturally. The word *compassion* means to suffer with. It is more than empathy or sympathy. A healthy marriage is filled with compassion. When a husband hurts, the wife also hurts. Likewise, when a wife is experiencing pain, the husband feels it too. The mutual love a husband and wife share in the Sacrament of Matrimony allows them to enter into one another's sufferings in a unique and special way. Compassion can get lost in our day-to-day interactions if we are not purposeful. We may answer our spouse sharply. We may not have the time or patience for their burdens because we have enough of our own. We forgo the little rituals of connection required to build our marriage, and slowly dismantle the relationship we cherish most instead. The beautiful thing about compassion is that when both spouses live it, the burdens we each carry become lighter and the future appears brighter, because we are truly living as one.

**Prayer:** Lord, may we never fail to be compassionate toward one another. Give us the grace to live as one. Amen.

# Day 252

*As life goes on, they become not two compatible beings*
*who have learned to live together through self-suppression*
*and patience, but one new and richer being, fused in the*
*fires of God's love and tempered of the best of both.*

— *Ven. Fulton J. Sheen*

Marriage is meant to be the most intimate and fulfilling relationship that two people can experience. When we marry, our spouse becomes a part of us. Just as we would protect and care for ourselves, we must do the same for our spouse. Learning to truly live as one does not happen instantly. After a husband and wife are joined in marriage, they are no longer two single individuals but one united couple. This is not to say that each person loses their individuality, but rather when we choose to join with another in marriage the focus changes from "me" and "mine," to "we" and "ours."

**Prayer:** Lord, united in you, help us live as truly one in every aspect of our lives. Amen.

# DAY 253

*Christians must lean on the Cross of Christ just as travelers lean on a staff when they begin a long journey.*

— *St. Anthony of Padua*

Marriage is a beautiful and exciting journey that begins the day we say, "I do."

I do promise to walk with you through welcoming life into this world, through weathering physical challenges, job uncertainties, and the loss of loved ones.

I do promise to be by your side through all of life's ups, downs, turns, and setbacks.

Along this journey, the Cross of Christ serves to provide a framework and support. It is through the power of the Cross that we experience salvation, know forgiveness, and discover hope. There is a very real spiritual war being waged against Christian marriage, but we can take authority through Christ's victory on the Cross against the evil forces that threaten us. Cling to the Cross always. Place a crucifix in a prominent place in your home as a reminder of the staff you need to make the journey.

**Prayer**: Lord, teach us how to lean on the Cross as we travel through life together. Amen.

# Day 254

*The family that prays together stays together.*

— *Bl. Patrick Peyton*

Prayer bonds couples and families like nothing else can. We can share meals together, recreate together, work together, and take trips together, but there is nothing stronger than the bond of prayer. Despite all the complexities of merging two lives into one and building a family together, the secret to staying closely knit is simple: Pray together. Go to Mass as a family, pray before meals as a family, pray the Rosary as a family, and pray for specific intentions and prayers of thanksgiving as a family. But be sure to pray together as a couple too. Make God the center of your domestic church and prayer a permanent fixture in your home.

**Prayer:** Lord, thank you for the gift of our family. Help us to form a lasting bond through prayer. Amen.

# Day 255

*To always be close to Jesus, that's my life plan. I'm happy to die because I've lived my life without wasting even a minute of it doing things that wouldn't have pleased God.*

*— Bl. Carlo Acutis*

Our friend, Guy, was a beloved husband and father of ten. His death left an enormous void in his family and among all who knew him. He lived his life completely for Jesus. As Kathleen drove by the funeral home for the first time since Guy's death, she was reminded of the fragility of life. We were just beginning to emerge from a drought in our marriage that had been the result of productivity driven by our collective ambitions, but which robbed us of necessary time for reflection, conversation, and just being together. Few of us can say that we didn't waste a minute on things that led us away from God. But we have limited time to do what is right. We don't know when God will call us home, so it is crucial to use the time we are given, each breath we are blessed to breathe, to prepare our hearts for eternal life with him.

**Prayer:** Lord, may we use each moment you give us to prepare our hearts for eternal life with you. Through our vocation to marriage, teach us how us to help one another reach heaven. Amen.

# Day 256

*Meet their angry outbursts with your own gentleness,*
*their boastfulness with your humility, their reviling's*
*with your prayers, their error with your constancy*
*in faith, their harshness with your meekness.*

— *St. Ignatius of Antioch*

The lotus blooms from the thickest and deepest mud. Once it emerges from the mud, breaks the surface of the water, and blooms, the lotus flower is entirely unmarked by the dirt that it came from. Like the lotus flower, we have the ability, through the gift of sacramental grace, to rise above the muddy parts of marriage and bloom despite the murky waters and darkness we may experience. We can utilize the grace of our sacrament to meet angry outbursts with kindness, pride with humility, error with faith, and harsh words with love. Being a faithful spouse does not mean we are required to fight every battle. Instead, we should choose our battles wisely and walk away when necessary. We trust God to cultivate beauty even when things are messy.

**Prayer:** Lord, we know that you can and will bring something beautiful out of the muddiest of situations. Help us trust you. Amen.

# DAY 257

*Conduct yourselves wisely towards outsiders,*
*making the most of the time.*

*— Colossians 4:5*

One holy marriage can touch more hearts than a million arguments or a thousand protest marches. Our marriages are living, breathing gospels — and we must have the courage to speak the good news well! Married couples, united in Christ, are desperately needed to rebuild our broken society, evangelize our distorted and godless culture, and uphold the true dignity of the sacrament to which we are called. We can do this by simply loving the way God asks us to love through the vocation of marriage. When others witness the sacrifices spouses make for each other, and when they see the passion we have to live our vocation well, they are often led to further explore the reason for our hope and joy. Take courage! When lived according to God's plan, marriage has the potential to transform the world.

**Prayer:** Lord, may we be a living example of a holy marriage in union with your divine plan for our lives.

# Day 258

*Every one to whom much is given, of*
*him will much be required.*

— *Luke 12:48*

We have this Scripture embroidered on a pillow we were given as a gift many years ago. It sat on a bench in our entryway for several years as a reminder to embrace each day as God gives it to us, the good, the bad, and everything in between. When we are faithful, God can count on us to receive whatever he gives and allow him to use it for good. God is never outdone in generosity, but from those to whom he has given much, he also expects much. Has God blessed your marriage? If so, allow God to work through you as a couple to show other married couples the beauty of sacrificial love lived out according to his plan. God wants your marriage to speak his truth to a world starving for authentic witnesses to the gift of sacramental marriage.

**Prayer:** Lord, help us to embrace whatever you send us. Use all that you give us for our good and the good of other married couples. Amen.

# DAY 259

*Do not be deceived; God is not mocked, for*
*whatever a man sows, that he will also reap.*

— *Galatians 6:7*

Early in our marriage, we lived in a quaint country town surrounded by farmland as far as the eye could see. Our rented home had two apricot trees in the backyard. Yet when spring came, only one tree budded, while the other appeared dormant. As summer approached, we grew excited to harvest the fruit from the single apricot tree that had bloomed, but no fruit came. The one tree that appeared dormant was actually dying. The other tree was able to stay alive and grow independently from the dying tree, but it needed the other apricot tree for cross-pollination.

So we decided to address the needs of the dying tree. We fertilized and watered it, then cleared away shrubs that were blocking the sunlight. The following spring, both trees bloomed! And as summer neared, fruit grew on both trees.

Marriage is like those two apricot trees. In order for a marriage to be strong and produce godly fruit, both souls must be alive in Christ, the root and the source of our sacramental grace. As marital love matures, the roots will grow deeper, and the fruit will become more abundant..

**Prayer:** Lord, help us remain united to you, the root of our love, so we may have a fruitful and abundant marriage. Amen.

# Day 260

*You must ask God to give you power to fight against the sin of pride which is your greatest enemy — the root of all that is evil, and the failure of all that good. For God resists the proud.*

— *St. Vincent de Paul*

In Kathleen's eyes, Troy is a superstar. He is incredibly talented, smart, thoughtful, and full of life. And yet, whenever he receives a compliment, he always points to God as the giver of all that he possesses. There is nothing more attractive to her than Troy's humility. In his humility, she sees God at work. Humility is to take our place in life gracefully. To recognize that every talent, gift, and blessing come from God and all glory must be given to him. When we have an elevated view of ourselves, it is often a sign that we do not comprehend our true identity and source of self-worth. When pride is present, intimacy is absent. Husbands and wives should always strive to be humble before God and one another.

**Prayer:** Lord, thank you for every gift, talent, and blessing. We pray for the grace of humility to use what you have given us for your glory. Amen.

# Day 261

*Our body has this defect that, the more it is provided*
*care and comforts, the more needs and desires it finds.*

— *St. Teresa of Ávila*

Our lives are full of luxuries and modern conveniences. Most of us have everything we need, and much of what we want. We might wonder why, with access to so much, there are so many divorces, suicides, violent crimes, and substance abuses. Scrolling all the way back to Adam and Eve, we can see that little has changed. They had *everything* they could want as well as intimacy with God, yet they still craved the forbidden fruit. Now how does this pertain to marriage? In marriage we are called to die to ourselves for the sake of our spouse and, if we are blessed with children, for our family. When we focus on acquiring more of what makes us comfortable in this life, we reveal our unwillingness to make sacrifices. Eventually, this unwillingness can become an inability to do without, even for the sake of someone we love.

**Prayer:** Lord, we know that peace and contentment are found in you alone. Keep us from becoming attached to the pleasures and comforts of earthly life. Amen.

# DAY 262

*When justice is done, it is a joy to the*
*righteous, but dismay to evildoers.*

*— Proverbs 21:15*

We should not attempt to pacify our spouse as a means of circumventing the pain we have caused them through our own sinfulness. Early on in our marriage, Troy let his pride get in the way of sincerely seeing his part in a problem. At times, he withheld justice from Kathleen and chose to placate her instead. What a spouse wants, needs, and deserves when an injustice has been done is recognition of the injustice and a sincere apology from the one who caused it. Justice is simply giving a person what is rightfully due to them. It isn't anything extra, but only the minimum required for any relationship to exist. There are no substitutes.

**Prayer:** Lord, help us practice both justice and charity in our marriage. When we fail, may we have the inner strength and humility to sincerely apologize. Amen.

# Day 263

*You have put off the old man with his practices and*
*have put on the new man, who is being renewed*
*in knowledge after the image of his creator.*

*— Colossians 3:9–10*

Have you ever noticed that the closer we get to a mirror, the more visibly we see our imperfections? If we stand back a few feet, we do not see our blemishes as clearly — or perhaps not even at all! God is like a mirror. The closer we come to him, the more clearly we see who we really are. Our faults and imperfections are magnified in the light of Christ. But if we refuse to see ourselves as we really are, we develop a false sense of pride. We will never be perfect this side of heaven, nor should we expect perfection from our spouse. But we are called to become fully who God created us to be. Only when we humbly recognize our inadequacies and failings can we fulfill the mission God gave us as husband and wife.

**Prayer:** Lord, give us the humility to see our own imperfections clearly. Amen.

# Day 264

*Give something, however small, to the one in need.*
*For it is not small to one who has nothing. Neither is*
*it small to God if we have given what we could.*

— *St. Gregory Nazianzen*

We should always strive to give our spouse our best, but the reality is we are often tired and feel as if we have nothing left to give. Sometimes giving the little we have can still go a long way. Once, Kathleen was swamped with a particular project. Those last few weeks before the project deadline, she was burning the candle at both ends. But Troy's workload also picked up and he too was staying up to all hours to meet everyone's needs. We were both exhausted and it showed. Nevertheless, Troy offered to give Kathleen a massage before we went to bed each night. He gave what little he had to Kathleen out of pure love and it made all the difference! It's important to give what we can, no matter how small it may be. The little things add up, and often mean more because the sacrifice required to offer them is greater.

**Prayer:** Lord, with your love, please help us give to one another whatever we are capable of giving without reserve. Amen.

# Day 265

*Bloom where you are planted.*

*— Attributed to St. Francis de Sales*

Moving from Illinois to South Carolina was a huge leap of faith for our family. Our roots were very strong, but when God made it clear that he was asking us to move, we uprooted our family in the middle of the pandemic and moved to Greenville, South Carolina. While God paved the path for us to relocate, working every detail out, it was up to us to do all the heavy lifting. When God says go, and we say yes, it is amazing to watch his plan unfold. We knew that we were selling our house in a difficult market, and yet we had forty showings in nine days, and three offers on our wedding anniversary! When God plants (or transplants!) us somewhere, he expects us to bloom. There were several purposes for our relocation, but the main reason was to assist at a Catholic Retreat Center in Sunset, South Carolina, doing marriage and family ministry. We have been in awe of how our marriage and family has blossomed since we moved south. We are grateful not only for God's invitation but for the grace to embrace it.

**Prayer:** Lord, help us to bloom where you plant us and to be open to your direction in our lives. Amen.

# Day 266

*Be souls of prayer. Never tire of praying, it is what is essential.*
*Prayer shakes the heart of God; it obtains necessary graces.*

— *St. Pio of Pietrelcina*

Prayer is our lifeline — both in our individual spiritual lives and in marriage. Prayer enlarges our heart and gives us the graces necessary to be faithful to our vocation. It can be hard to know where to start, but prayer is simply talking with God, either aloud or in the silence of the heart. We can tell God what's on our mind, and thank him for his blessings. We can ask him to help us with our struggles and praise him for his sacrifice on the cross. We can seek his blessing for our marriage and family. If spontaneous prayer is uncomfortable, formal prayer is good too. Pray an Our Father, or a decade of the Rosary. We should start where we are comfortable and continue the journey until we discover what kind of prayer is best suited to our personality and where we are in life. The single most important thing is showing up.

**Prayer:** Lord, help us take time each day to connect with you in prayer. Amen.

# Day 267

*And he came to the disciples and found them sleeping; and he said to Peter, "So, could you not watch with me one hour?"*

— *Matthew 26:40*

We cannot live our faith without community. To follow the will of the Father requires a support system of like-minded believers. Jesus surrounded himself with a community of disciples. In marriage, we should surround ourselves with other couples who are striving to fully live their vocation in union with Christ and the Church's teachings. Who is your support system? Who holds you accountable?

One of the first things we did when we relocated to South Carolina was seek community. Kathleen joined a women's group and Troy joined a men's group. We connected our children through youth group and other parish ministries. God did not intend for us to do marriage and family life alone. It's important to have the support system we need to faithfully live our vocation.

**Prayer:** Lord, please provide us with faithful friends and community to support us in our journey. Amen.

# DAY 268

*The joy of the LORD is your strength.*

*— Nehemiah 8:10*

A few years ago, Kathleen's spiritual director asked her to come up with three concrete ways God had shown his love to her in the previous week. Her mind immediately flooded with the basics: He gave her life, health, a beautiful family, community. But coming up with three specific ways challenged her to go deeper. This simple exercise made us both realize that if we were more mindful of God's active presence in our lives moment to moment, our hearts would be filled with joy. Imagine what a game-changer it would be if we were more mindful of God's active presence in our marriage? Joy would radiate even in the most difficult of times because we would be aware of God's hand at work molding and creating something beautiful in the midst of the messy.

**Prayer:** Lord, may we always be mindful of your active presence in our lives and in our marriage. Amen.

# Day 269

*Why do you see the speck that is in your brother's eye,*
*but do not notice the log that is in your own eye? Or how*
*can you say to your brother, "Brother, let me take out the*
*speck that is in your eye," when you yourself do not see*
*the log that is in your own eye? You hypocrite, first take*
*the log out of your own eye, and then you will see clearly*
*to take out the speck that is in your brother's eye.*

— *Luke 6:41–42*

One of the most powerful prayers married men and women can pray is the transformative prayer, "Lord change me." Our immediate and natural response when we feel hurt or frustrated with our spouse is usually, "God please change them." But it is always best to ask, "Lord, what do I need to change to be a better spouse, a more supportive and loving husband or wife?"

**Prayer:** Lord, please show us each what we need to change to be the husband and wife that you are calling us to be. Amen.

# Day 270

*A friend loves at all times.*

*— Proverbs 17:17*

After our son Dominic suddenly died at four months old, another parent who had also lost a child to Sudden Infant Death Syndrome said, "The deeper you love, the greater the loss." We have often reflected on these words of wisdom, especially during the painful seasons of our marriage. The more we love, the more painful it is when the one we love hurts or leaves us. This is not to say that it is better to never have loved, for in loving we truly live. But loving another person requires risk. This is where sacramental grace comes in as our greatest resource in marriage, to heal the wounds that we inevitably cause each other and to press into the pain to move forward toward greater love and union in our marriage.

**Prayer:** Lord, may we never fear growing in our love for one another out of fear of possible pain. Amen.

# DAY 271

*He has showed you, O man, what is good;*
*and what does the LORD require of you*
*but to do justice, and to love kindness,*
*and to walk humbly with your God?*

— *Micah 6:8*

Giving in to get along in marriage is not a healthy strategy. Too often we are eager to end tension because we simply don't want to deal with the soul work involved to work through a disagreement. It is good and gracious to be accommodating to the preferences of our spouse in certain circumstances, and it is good to serve. But if one spouse always gives and the other always takes, major problems are likely to arise. In a strong marriage both spouses give and take. Yielding may appear like the right thing to do in the moment to achieve peace, but usually this peace is temporary and superficial. Instead, learn to live with a certain degree of tension. It is always best to take the time we need to understand our own and our spouse's motives.

**Prayer:** Lord, please help us both to give and take in our marriage so we can live a full and balanced life as one united in you. Amen.

# DAY 272

*The memory of the righteous is a blessing.*

— *Proverbs 10:7*

W hen Kathleen is feeling down or having a difficult day, she looks at the pictures on her phone to recall better days. She has made albums of each of our children and also of her favorite pictures of time she's spent with Troy. Looking at this album reminds her of all the special moments we have shared together, the beautiful life we have built, and the family we have co-created together with God. A few years ago, when Troy was in Costa Rica on a business trip, we were struggling to emotionally connect. His frequent international travel had begun to take a toll on our marriage. Kathleen decided to text him some photos. As memory after memory came through on Troy's phone, he found it hard to ignore them, despite feeling distant. So he finally gave in and entered into the pictures. He called Kathleen that night and, through tears, we prayed together and reconciled. The fond memories broke through our darkness.

**Prayer:** Lord, when darkness creeps into our marriage, may we fondly recall and find hope in the light of brighter days. Amen.

# DAY 273

*Nothing great is ever achieved without enduring much.*

— *St. Catherine of Siena*

"No pain, no gain," so the saying goes. If we want to attain a fruitful and happy marriage, then we must be willing to put in the effort and work through the painful times. One evening several years ago, we were struggling through a disagreement, so we decided to call a timeout. Kathleen left the house and went to the gym, hoping to relieve stress and gain a new perspective. But when she got there, she struggled to get out of the car and go in. Eventually, she forced herself to run through the rain from the back of the parking lot to the gym door. Once in and dry, she decided to lift weights. As she pushed the weights up and felt the burning in her arms, she prayed that God would push the fear out of her heart and replace it with a renewed burning and yearning to do his will in our marriage. That night was a turning point in our marriage.

**Prayer:** Lord, we know that good things do not come easily. Give us the grace we need to put in the effort and push through our pain. Amen.

# DAY 274

*There is no fear in love, but perfect love casts out fear.*

— *1 John 4:18*

Have you ever observed how freely children love? Their trusting hearts allow them to give themselves fearlessly and without reserve. Our more mature hearts have been tainted by sin, injured by others, and crushed under the weight of day-to-day stresses. Perhaps that's why we hesitate when it comes to loving our spouse without reserve. One romantic tune that expresses how we are to love our spouse is "All of Me," by John Legend. Definitely one of our favorites! When we love without reserve, we make ourselves vulnerable to pain and disappointment. Love completely, nevertheless. Be vulnerable. When we take the risk to love beyond our comfort zone, we learn how to love more completely.

**Prayer:** Lord, help us to love one another without reserve and have the courage to be vulnerable in our marriage. Amen.

# Day 275

*Happiness does not depend on accumulating*
*more things, but on the mindset we have*
*concerning the things we already do possess.*

— *Ven. Fulton J. Sheen*

When preparing to move, we went through box after box of stuff and filtered through what to keep and what to let go of. The process was a trip down memory lane and a good reminder of how much we possessed in rich memories, but also how much we literally possessed. As we decluttered, we began to discover the truth in the phrase, "Less is more." Less is more because there is not as much to take care of and clean, we can find things more quickly, we stay more organized, our home looks and feels more spacious and peaceful, and we have more mental capacity to devote to the accumulation of wonderful memories rather than physical objects. There is nothing wrong with having a lot of things or finding delight them. What is wrong is when our happiness is dependent upon what we accumulate.

**Prayer:** Lord, help us to be grateful and content with what we have and keep us from becoming too attached to material things. Amen.

# DAY 276

*We will either accuse ourselves or excuse ourselves.*

— *St. John Vianney*

When we address difficulties in marriage, we have a choice to either "accuse" ourselves or "excuse" ourselves. Do we take blame for whatever is wrong or justify whatever we do with excuses? Being honest about ourselves and with our spouse is key to building a strong marriage. But most of us tend to gravitate to one of these two unhealthy options. There are better choices. Instead of thinking of ourselves as either someone who can do no wrong or someone who can't do anything right, we can seek a deeper knowledge of who we really are. Knowing ourselves is the basis for real growth. When we know ourselves, we can accept our faults and take responsibility for them without losing hope. When we know ourselves, we can stop being defensive and learn to see the real consequences of our actions without feeling condemned. We've found that when we accept our faults, take ownership for our actions and bring our imperfections to Christ, real growth occurs, and we become free to support growth in each other as well.

**Prayer:** Lord, may we come to know who we truly are in you, so we can be honest and forthright in all our actions and open to your transforming grace. Amen.

# DAY 277

*Two are better than one, because they have a good*
*reward for their toil. For if they fall, one will lift*
*up his fellow; but woe to him who is alone when*
*he falls and has not another to lift him up.*

— *Ecclesiastes 4:9–10*

One of the greatest blessings in marriage is the holy partnership that spouses share. United we stand strong, even if one of us falls. We are motivated to work together when we disagree, to find a solution where there are no winners or losers. When one of us is having a tough day, we have the benefit of our spouse's support and encouragement. If we are sick, our spouse can pick up the slack and help care for our needs. If we lose a job, a spouse can temporarily carry the weight. If we are mistreated, our spouse is right there to remind us of our worth. Two really are better than one.

**Prayer:** Lord, thank you for the blessing of our holy partnership in marriage. Please give us the grace to live it each day according to your design. Amen.

# Day 278

*Whereas the aim of our charge is love that issues from a pure heart and a good conscience and sincere faith.*

— *1 Timothy 1:5*

Do we give our spouse credit for good intentions, even if the result is not what we imagined or desired? When we fail to acknowledge our spouse's efforts, it is discouraging to him or her. It also demotivates our spouse to do anything kind or thoughtful in the future. Instead, we should give credit for our spouse's good intentions. And if we have forgiven an offense, we should never throw it back in our spouse's face. Instead, choose to think well of the one we married. When we do, we will usually find them living up to how we see them.

**Prayer:** Lord, may we always recognize and give credit to each other for good intentions. Help us to see one another in the most positive light. Amen.

# DAY 279

*Confession heals, confession justifies, confession grants*
*pardon of sin. All hope consists in confession.*

— *St. Isidore of Seville*

W hen we begin to feel hopeless in our marriage, remember that "all hope consists in confession." True remission of sin gives us a clean slate to start over and the grace to make progress in virtue. As a family we try to make monthly confession a staple, and we celebrate it! After confession, we usually take the kids out for ice cream or a treat of some sort. A healthy marriage necessitates frequent confession. The Sacrament of Reconciliation retunes our marriage and gives us the grace to say, "I am sorry" and "I forgive you" — two of the most powerful and life-giving phrases we can say to someone we love.

**Prayer:** Lord, thank you for the gift of your forgiveness through the Sacrament of Reconciliation. Give us the grace to extend the mercy we receive from you to one another. Amen.

# Day 280

*The revival of the Rosary in Christian families,*
*within the context of a broader pastoral ministry to*
*the family, will be an effective aid to countering the*
*devastating effects of this crisis typical of our age.*

— *Pope St. John Paul II*

A friend recently shared that she began praying the Rosary every night a little over a year ago. At first her husband was resentful since it took away from time they could be spending together, but two months into her nightly routine, he reluctantly began joining her. Now, a year later, her marriage is more dynamic and stronger than ever. There is peace in her home, and both she and her husband look forward to their nightly Rosary together. Prayer is powerful, and the Rosary is a beautiful form of prayer. We should consider making the Rosary a part of our daily routine, even if it's just one decade a day. Look for pockets of time when we can make it part of our day. If we can pray together as a couple or family, even better!

**Prayer:** Lord, thank you for the gift of the Rosary. Help us integrate it into our life together. Amen.

# DAY 281

*Thank God ahead of time.*

— *Bl. Solanus Casey*

Finances, children, aging parents, jobs, life-altering decisions, health issues — there's a lot we are expected to juggle and manage. These things can begin to weigh us down if we don't keep our heads up and focused on the God who's got our back. When we are finally able to look back and see the big picture, we'll know how God wove every detail of our life together to create a beautiful masterpiece. Until that day, we are called to trust in the end result and to thank God "ahead of time." Thank him for our present reality, thank him for whatever our future holds, thank him for the answered prayers, and even thank him for the unanswered prayers. There is always a reason to thank God.

**Prayer:** Lord, thank you for what you have done, what you are doing now and what you will do in the future in our marriage. Amen.

# DAY 282

*For everything there is a season, and a time*
*for every matter under heaven.*

— *Ecclesiates 3:1*

One of our family's favorite summer activities is swimming in our backyard pool. Troy works hard to maintain the appropriate chemical balance, and often refers to it as one big chemistry experiment. Marriage can also sometimes seem like one big chemistry experiment. The "chemistry" we share can easily get off-balance. The first step to creating and maintaining balance is ensuring that priorities are correctly ordered: God first, marriage second, children third, and work fourth. Life circumstances might require a temporary shift in focus, but not a rearranging of priorities.

We shouldn't be ashamed or embarrassed if outside intervention is needed to cultivate a healthier marriage. Many couples are not fully equipped with the necessary tools, or need help to overcome lingering hurts or dysfunction. We may need a few minor adjustments to get back on track, but sometimes the entire pool may need to be emptied. Whatever the case, dive in and get to work either to strengthen or to restore balance in your marriage.

**Prayer:** Lord, help us to create and maintain good "chemistry" in our marriage. Amen.

# Day 283

*Do not fear what may happen tomorrow; the same understanding father who cares for you today will take care of you then and every day. He will either shield you from suffering or will give you unfailing strength to bear it. Be at peace and put aside all anxious thoughts and imaginations.*

— *St. Francis de Sales*

Marriage is a life-giving, unbreakable covenant, not a contract that comes with limited liability. A contract is conditional and built on a foundation of distrust. It is a written agreement outlining the consequences to be applied if the contract is broken. A covenant on the other hand is built on a foundation of total trust. It is a commitment that assures your spouse that your promise is unconditional, sacramental, and good for a lifetime. It is important to evaluate what our mindset looked like at the beginning of our marriage. Did we go into marriage thinking that divorce was a possible out? Are we currently living marriage with a contract or covenant approach? We need not fear the future. God will never abandon us but will always see us through. In marriage, we are called to love each other with that kind of fidelity.

**Prayer:** Lord, help us to always live our sacramental marriage with a covenant mindset. Amen.

# DAY 284

*By [the Sacrament of Matrimony], husband and wife*
*are strengthened and . . . consecrated for the faithful*
*accomplishment of their proper duties, for the carrying out*
*of their proper vocation even to perfection, and the Christian*
*witness which is proper to them before the whole world.*

— *Pope St. Paul VI*

The vow married couples make to love each other "in sickness" is eventually called into action and often tested in a big way. For Steve and Jeanette, it happened when she was diagnosed with a brain tumor twenty-seven years into their marriage. God's love became acutely tangible through Steve, as he cared for his beloved during this uncertain and painful season. For Jeanette, the most powerful memory of this agonizing time is that of her husband helping her walk into the hospital on the morning of her surgery with two backpacks of belongings in tow. It was as if he carried the weight of the cross on his shoulders. By the sacramental grace of their marriage, Steve was empowered to carry out his vocation, beautifully modeling Christ's love for Jeanette in her time of need.

**Prayer:** Lord, help us draw from the wellspring of grace you provide for us so we may faithfully carry out our duties as husband and wife. Amen.

# DAY 285

*Through love be servants of one another.*

— *Galatians 5:13*

As Kathleen wipes the kitchen counter for what seems like the one hundredth time, or rinses each plate after every meal, or washes the pile of clothes spilling out of the laundry room, she tries to remember that it is these ordinary moments each day that God wants to make extraordinary through the love he asks her to pour into each task. A messy counter means we are blessed with a home and a family to love; dirty plates testify that we have food to eat; the mountain of soiled clothes is a sign that God had provided for our family's needs. We are called to serve our family through these simple tasks each day — not because we love the tasks, but because we love the people for whom we are doing them. Our example of loving mutual service as husbands and wives sets the tone of the home.

**Prayer:** Lord, help us each to have a servant's heart, especially within the walls of our home. Amen.

# Day 286

*If families give Our Lady fifteen minutes a day by reciting the Rosary, I assure them that their homes will become, by God's grace, peaceful places.*

— *Ven. Father Patrick Peyton*

We have prayed the Rosary on and off as a family, but not consistently until the last few years. The difference it has made in the overall atmosphere of our home is so significant that we could never go back to making it a prayer to fit in when we can. It is not that we didn't know about the power of the Rosary or the incredible spiritual weapon it is. We simply never grasped the depth of what we had heard from those who had experienced the same results we now know to be true. We are thankful we finally made our fifteen minute Rosary a daily priority. While it is not always practical for all of us to be together, those who can pray together do. We find a way to make it work because we don't want to miss out on all the beautiful blessings we have received by doing it.

**Prayer:** Lord, help us make it a priority to pray the Rosary together as often as possible to receive the blessings you desire to shower upon us through this beautiful prayer. Amen.

# Day 287

*Move on!*

*— Attributed to St. Joan of Arc*

Many times, we must shift to plan B when things don't go the way we expect or hope they will. A few years ago, Kathleen arrived at the gym and put our then three-year-old in babysitting. After ten minutes, she was contacted and told that she needed to come get him. She headed home and called Troy, who was sitting on a plane ready to take off for a business trip. "I can't even go for a walk because it is negative 4 outside!" she complained. Troy calmed Kathleen down and helped her refocus. Later, as she reflected on the day, Kathleen realized she was wearing a shirt with these words spoken by St. Joan of Arc, "Move on!" How many times are we called to move on? Move on from an addiction that is holding us back? Move on from a relationship that is pulling us down? Move on from pain that prevents us from growing? Move on from fear that holds us back from our goals? Saint Joan of Arc got it. She knew that in life it is necessary to move on if we are to be the person God created us to be.

**Prayer:** Lord, when life does not go according to our plans, please help us to trust your plan and move on. Amen.

# Day 288

*The perfection of moral virtue does not wholly
take away the passions but regulates them.*

— *St. Thomas Aquinas*

Our passions are neither good nor bad in and of themselves. They can motivate us to do good works, but they may also drive us to engage in sinful behaviors if not properly regulated through virtue. Mismanaged and distorted passions can do extensive damage to a marriage. If we let our passions control us, instead of us being in control of them, we become their slaves instead of their masters, and our marriage suffers. Passions are corrupted by bad habits and vices. But when our passions are governed by our well-formed reason, good habits and virtues are formed and God can work through our passions in incredible ways. When a couple learns self-control and unites their passions for good, God can do amazing things.

**Prayer:** Lord, help us be master of our passions and use them for your glory and the salvation of our souls. Amen.

# Day 289

*Now there are varieties of gifts, but the same Spirit; and
there are varieties of service, but the same Lord.*

— *1 Corinthians 12:4–5*

Sometimes it's hard for spouses to remember that we are on the same team. United, we have the power to set the world on fire with the unique gifts, experiences, and resources we each bring to the table. Marriage must be complementary rather than competitive. God brings a man and woman together in marriage with each of their strengths and weaknesses, knowing full well how they will complement one another in cooperation with his grace. Throughout the course of our marriage, we have had a few occasions where our roles have been temporarily reversed. It is in these moments that we have both grown in respect for one another and appreciation of what each of us can and cannot do, and we've been granted new insight into what we can accomplish together. When a husband and wife join forces and draw strength from their sacramental grace, amazing things can happen.

**Prayer:** Lord, help us not to be envious of the gifts or opportunities you have given our spouse, but rather see them as a call to serve you and one another. Amen.

# Day 290

*We must sometimes bear with little defects in others, as*
*we have, against our will, to bear with natural defects*
*in ourselves. If we wish to keep peace with our neighbor,*
*we should never remind anyone of his natural defects.*

— *St. Philip Neri*

No one's perfect. We both have faults. It does no good for either of us to keep tabs on each other's weaknesses, nor highlight each other's mistakes. Those who spend time looking for faults in others usually spend little time correcting their own. God reserves the right to change our spouse; it is not our right or responsibility. If something is a serious concern, we must approach it in love. Let our spouse know how their defect is affecting us. Be accountable to one another and patient as we both work through our weakness. We should avoid projecting our own faults onto our spouse and blaming them for our sinful behaviors. Finally, we must always strive to practice mercy in marriage.

**Prayer:** Lord, help us practice mercy in our marriage and be patient with one another's flaws. Amen.

# DAY 291

*Blessed is the one who does not speak through hope of reward,*
*who is not always ready to unburden himself of his secrets,*
*who is not anxious to speak, but who reflects prudently on*
*what he is to say and the manner in which he is to reply.*

— *St. Francis of Assisi*

How often do we compose a reply to our spouse in our heads while they are still speaking, instead of truly listening to what they have to say and then formulating a response? We are often so anxious to speak and make our own opinion known that we miss out on what our spouse is trying to communicate to us in the moment. Healthy communication requires that we truly listen. It also requires that we prudently reflect on what we want to communicate and then purposely and prayerfully choose the appropriate words and tone of voice to convey that message to our spouse. In marriage, we do well to say less and listen more.

**Prayer:** Lord, please help us to develop healthy listening skills in our marriage. Amen.

# DAY 292

*You cannot please both God and the world at the*
*same time. They are utterly opposed to each other in*
*their thoughts, their desires, and their actions.*

— *St. John Vianney*

As lay people striving to live the Christian life within the Sacrament of Matrimony, it is challenging to find a healthy balance between living in the world, but not of the world. We need to do what is necessary to provide for our family, but remain cautious not to compromise our values. In Troy's line of work as a businessman, he frequently travels for his job. He is blessed to stay in upscale hotels and eat at some of the finest restaurants all over the country and occasionally in other countries. This may sound enticing — and it is. Consequently, Troy knows that he must be focused in faith and grounded in values so he can be purposeful in his decisions and actions. Sometimes he has lost his balance and focus. The good news is that God is merciful, and Kathleen is patient. Through his own failures and successes, Troy has learned to stay vigilant and keep his heart united to Christ!

**Prayer:** Lord, when we are allured by the ways of the world, please rescue us from the traps that lead to emptiness and help us fix our eyes on you. Amen.

# DAY 293

*I am the Lord your God, who brought you up out of the*
*land of Egypt. Open your mouth wide, and I will fill it.*

*— Psalm 81:10*

As a busy mom of four, Lisa strives to keep her marriage a priority but admits it can often be challenging. She recalls how one day she became keenly aware that she was not meeting her husband's needs. It was the end of a long day, which included a wonderful family party, when Lisa asked her children if anyone else needed something to eat. All four of her kiddos neglected to respond but her husband chimed in, "I'd like to eat!" She laughed, but then realized that he was hungry. In the bustle of serving everyone else, she had forgotten to serve him. Husbands need their wives — not in a dysfunctional way, but in a healthy, holy way. Our husbands need us to cheer them on, convey our need for them, care for their hearts, provide comfort, and regularly consummate our love. God provides for our spouse, but often he does so through our vocation as husbands and wives.

**Prayer:** Lord, give us the grace each day to embrace our responsibility as husbands and wives to care for one another's needs. Amen.

# Day 294

*Good things poured out upon a mouth that is closed*
*are like offerings of food placed upon a grave.*

— *Sirach 30:18*

Have you ever felt like the words "I love you" fell on deaf ears? Often our spouse cannot receive the love we are attempting to give because of a wound we have inflicted. If we gloss over hurtful behavior, pretending as if it did not happen, and then we attempt to love our spouse, our love cannot be entirely received. The heart often closes when it is wounded. Recognition of any pain we may have caused, combined with a sincere apology, has the power to reopen the heart to receive love. Ask God for the grace to see clearly and be the bigger person, so the good we pour out can be received by the one we love.

**Prayer:** Lord, help us be aware of how we hurt one another and quick to apologize. Help us to keep our own hearts open and love in a way that opens our hearts to one another. Amen.

# Day 295

*Hear the other side.*

— *St. Augustine of Hippo*

We would add *listen* to the other side. All too often we hear what our spouse has to say, but we don't really listen. We have our own preconceived ideas and opinions that can get in the way of truly listening to our spouse and sincerely attempting to understand where they are coming from. So, let's put our preconceived opinions aside and open our heart to really enter into what our spouse is sharing with us. In a disagreement, there are always at least two sides to the story. We may think we are the one in the right, but that does not necessarily mean we are. First, take time to listen and understand what we are each communicating. If disagreement remains and there is no resolution, then agree to disagree and move on.

**Prayer:** Lord, may we truly listen with an open heart and mind to what our spouse has to say. Amen.

# Day 296

*Commit your work to the LORD,*
*and your plans will be established.*

— *Proverbs 16:3*

L ife is busy and demanding. There are ceaseless distractions that have the potential to lure us away from our most important role in life as a husband or wife. The key is to keep our gaze on God so that we do not lose sight of our vocation and the daily responsibility to love our spouse well. We have had our share of stretches where we have temporarily shifted our focus from one another in order to give more time and attention to work, the children, a pending project, or a health issue. A short-lived shift is sometimes necessary, but we must never neglect our marriage. When possible, we try and focus on what comes our way as a couple. Life is better when we conquer each task and challenge together. If a situation necessitates a shift in focus, be quick to re-focus on what is most valuable in life — namely, faith and the vocation to marriage. The longer we stray from what's most important, the more effort will be required to regain our focus.

**Prayer:** Lord, may we never lose sight of you or the vocation you have called us to live. Amen.

# Day 297

*People travel to wonder at the height of the mountains. At the huge waves of the seas. At the long course of the rivers. At the vast compass of the ocean. At the circular motion of the stars, and yet they pass by themselves without wondering.*

*— St. Augustine of Hippo*

When we were dating, we attended a mutual friend's wedding in Kansas City, Missouri. The day before the wedding we went to a nature preserve to see some of the local natural beauty. We sat for quite a while on a park bench in a gazebo talking. As Kathleen shared from her heart her dreams and goals, Troy listened intently. He was focused solely on her in that moment, not his job, not what we were going to do next, not the impending rain, just Kathleen. We were in wonder at the beauty we had found, not just in nature, but in each other.

**Prayer:** Lord, keep us from losing the sense of wonder we hold for each other. Amen.

# DAY 298

*He who does not love does not know God; for God is love.*

*— 1 John 4:8*

We are all born with a capacity to love and to receive love; and we learn how to love by knowing God and by simply loving. There is no other way to learn. We can read stacks of books and do all kinds of marriage enrichment activities. But loving each other well comes in time and with practice. We will make mistakes along the way, but if we do not give up, we will learn how to love just as we learn any other skill. Learning to love demands hands-on, on-the-job training.

**Prayer:** Lord, help us learn to love one another, not in theory, but in truth. Teach us to practice love always. Amen.

# Day 299

*The Cross symbolises the life of an apostle of Christ, with*
*a strength and a truth that delight both soul and body,*
*though sometimes it is hard, and we can feel its weight.*

— *St. Josemaría Escrivá*

A few years ago, Troy traveled extensively to San Jose, Costa Rica, for business. With very little time between trips to reconnect, there were numerous miscommunications, misunderstandings, and misperceptions that transpired. It was a long and bumpy stretch for our marriage. We experienced many desert moments with respect to feeling loved and cherished. Throughout that period, Kathleen frequently reminded herself, when you really love, no sacrifice is hard. Yet it *was* hard, and it *is* hard. This is where sacramental grace kicks in.

Utilize the grace of the sacrament, especially during the difficult seasons of marriage. With sacramental grace, we can march on in faith, strive to love more selflessly, practice mortification when we are tempted to stubbornly uphold our opinion, and sacrifice for our beloved. Our mission in marriage is to chip away at the flaws we have so we can more perfectly love God through loving our spouse.

**Prayer:** Lord, we come before you as two broken individuals yearning to love deeper. Help us freely sacrifice for one another with the help of our sacramental grace. Amen.

# DAY 300

*Above all, one must always be ready*
*for the Lord's surprise moves.*

— *Pope St. John XXIII*

We never cease to be amazed at God's work in our marriage when we let him take the reins. God is a God of surprises, and we have seen over and over again how he works all things for good. Through surprise crosses and moments of deep pain, we have learned to trust God's plan more deeply. In joyful surprises we have seen that God is never outdone in generosity. Finally, there are the surprises that, while neither painful nor joyful, impact our marriage and shift our course as we move on, trusting in God's will. The life of faith is quite an adventure. God is working in our lives and marriages all the time, and he wants to amaze us in ways that turn our hearts towards him. Be open to his surprises and embrace the journey.

**Prayer:** Lord, help us be ready for our next surprise from you and fully willing to embrace your work in our lives. Amen.

# DAY 301

*Toward the heights.*

— *Bl. Pier Giorgio Frassati*

Have you ever been tempted to give up on your marriage? When we struggle, many of us entertain the worldly mentality of instant gratification, data on demand, and the notion that if we're not getting what we need from our spouse now, we never will. But Christ calls us to a lifelong commitment of spousal union when we exchange our vows at the altar. The Sacrament of Matrimony is an invitation to ascend the heights of holiness through faithful commitment to the vows we made on our wedding day. Through each act of love and sacrifice made, we climb to greater heights of sanctity. God cares about every detail of our life and marriage, and it is in the details that he works and gently leads us forward on the path toward heaven.

**Prayer:** Lord, please help us ascend the heights of holiness through the everyday details of our marital life together. Amen.

# DAY 302

*Only the nakedness that turns the woman into an "object"*
*for the man, or vice versa, is a source of shame. The fact that*
*"they did not feel shame" [in the Garden of Eden] means that*
*the woman was not an "object" for the man, nor he for her.*

— *Pope St. John Paull II*

Gentlemen, how often have we lusted after our wife? We're in the mood, the urge sets in, and no matter what she tries to communicate to us, we can think of only one thing. We've all been there at one time or another. And the same can be said of a lustful woman for her man. St. John Paul II reminds us that it's only because of the Fall that we objectify our spouse. God never intended marriage to be this way. Instead, he intended for us to see beyond the physical and into our spouse's heart, which reflects, like a mirror, God in whose very image we are made. It is often said that the eye is the portal to the soul. That's because we're called to go deeper, beyond the external veneer, to see God alive in our spouse.

**Prayer:** Lord, when we are tempted to view one another as an object for our own pleasure, purify our thoughts and illuminate our vision to see each other through eyes of faith. Amen.

# DAY 303

*Love one another with brotherly affection;*
*outdo one another in showing honor.*

*— Romans 12:10*

It can be tempting to fake affection for our spouse in order to get something we want. Life gets busy, we have a need we want met, we don't feel like taking time to pour love into the moment, so we resort to charm to get what we want. Whether we are the one resorting to this immature action, or we are on the receiving end, we both walk away feeling empty. God calls us to a higher standard. Our love for our spouse must be sincere if we want them to feel loved for who they truly are. Respect and honor are at the heart of what makes a man feel loved. Dishonor results in serious damage. It is our duty as wives to help our husbands grasp how valuable they are through the delight we take in honoring and respecting them. Men, don't make this hard. Lead lives worthy of respect. Likewise, it is a husband's duty to show genuine affection for his wife so she knows she is loved through and through. Ladies, live with dignity. It is attractive and will draw your husband to you.

**Prayer:** Lord, help us love one another with genuine affection and take delight in honoring each other. Amen.

# DAY 304

*Be at peace; what God has started, He will finish.*

— *St. Maria Faustina Kowalska*

Saint Faustina reminds us that, despite the ups and downs of married life, God asks us to trust him. We can be at peace knowing that what he has started in our marriages, he will complete, if we cooperate with his will. God brought us together, united us in the Sacrament of Matrimony, and has a specific plan for our life together. He sees the good, the bad, and the apathy. But through adversity we grow in character, which fortifies us for the journey of marriage. Marriage is not an all-out sprint, but a paced marathon to fulfill our role on earth to love and serve him.

**Prayer:** Lord, help us be at peace and trust that what you have begun in us as a couple, united in the Sacrament of Matrimony, you will bring to completion for your greater glory. Amen.

# DAY 305

*Keep your life free from love of money, and be*
*content with what you have; for he has said,*
*"I will never fail you nor forsake you."*

— *Hebrews 13:5*

Some of our dearest friends have six boys and one girl, a total of nine people, and they live in a home of less than 1,000 square feet. Despite their lack of space, they frequently have company and use the little they do have to bless others. Their children do not complain about what they don't have. Instead, they are grateful to have a roof over their heads and live in a home filled with love. These friends are one of the most joyful and giving families we have been blessed to know. On the contrary, we also know several families who live in 6,000-plus square foot homes and are some of the most unhappy, discontented people we have ever encountered. The value of our life does not depend on where we live or what we have, but on how we use what we have been given. We must be careful not to fall prey to the "more is better" mentality, because often "more" is never enough. We cannot buy happiness.

**Prayer:** Lord, help us to be content with what we have and use whatever you give us with generosity. Amen.

# Day 306

*Never call her by her name alone, but with terms of endearment, honor, and love. … Prefer her before all others, both for her beauty and her discernment, and praise her.*

— *St. John Chrysostom*

When Kathleen hears Troy call her "honey," it warms her heart. There is something endearing about calling our beloved a special nickname. It helps to foster the affection that belongs to a loving and healthy marriage. Do we prefer each other's company before spending time alone or with others? It is natural and healthy to desire time alone and to want our own space in marriage. But if we don't long to spend time with our spouse, it's time to evaluate what is causing a lack of interest. Perhaps walls have been built through hurt or a lack of forgiveness. Or maybe rather than attracting our spouse, we are pushing them away. Whatever the case, God created us to long for our spouse and desire their company. We must cultivate an environment where love can freely grow and be expressed.

**Prayer:** Lord, keep us from taking each other for granted and help us to cherish and honor the gift we are to one another with affection. Amen.

# DAY 307

*The state of marriage is one that requires more*
*virtue and constancy than any other; it is a*
*perpetual exercise in mortification.*

— *St. Francis de Sales*

Mortification means to practice disciplines that bring death to one's disordered bodily desires. Notice that St. Francis de Sales indicates that marriage is a "perpetual" — that is, never-ending — exercise in mortification. Why? Because we are flawed and imperfect, and, therefore, prone to fall to worldly temptation every day. To be skilled at mortification in marriage, we must work daily at growing in virtue and building our spiritual armor to withstand temptations when they arise. When both spouses strive selflessly to live their lives for the Lord, and frequent the Sacrament of Reconciliation, the Holy Spirit will foster virtue and constancy between them. Marriage can make us holy if we embrace the countless opportunities for mortification that accompany it.

**Prayer:** Lord, help us grow in virtue so our marriage can bring us to holiness. Amen.

# DAY 308

*Do you really want to be a saint? Carry out the*
*little duty of each moment: do what you ought*
*and put yourself into what you are doing.*

— *St. Josemaría Escrivá*

There is nothing wrong with not wanting to do something that must be done, but each duty we are asked to fulfill gives us an opportunity to become a saint. In marriage, we are daily provided with ways to love through the little. Whether that is taking the garbage out, cleaning up broken glass, cutting the grass, setting up a necessary appointment, or running an unplanned errand, our duties can become our pathway to holiness. When Troy lovingly does a chore Kathleen knows he does not enjoy doing, she feels immense love for him. She knows that his willingness to do it anyway is an act of love. Through faithfulness to our daily responsibilities, love grows. And the more we lovingly give ourselves to the little each day, the more love we receive.

**Prayer:** Lord, thank you for the opportunity to become a saint! Please give us the grace necessary each day to be faithful to our duties and to do them in love. Amen.

# Day 309

*I am the vine, you are the branches. He who abides*
*in me, and I in him, he it is that bears much fruit,*
*for apart from me you can do nothing.*

— *John 15:5*

Healthy and well-fertilized branches produce fruit that eventually ripens, becoming tender and sweet to eat. However, undernourished branches either break from the vine or bear fruit that never fully ripens. The same can be said of a healthy marriage. Christ is the vine, and we are only the branches. We need the vine to survive, even if in our selfish, fallen state we may think we don't. When we are connected to him, our marriage is properly nourished and will bear fruit. When we try to go it alone and are not united to Christ, we lose the source of love for marriage.

**Prayer:** Lord, help us to continually remain connected to you as a couple, so our marriage may bear abundant fruit. Amen.

# Day 310

*If a man and a woman marry in order to be*
*companions on the journey to heaven, then*
*their union will bring them great joy.*

— *St. John Chrysostom*

God has a plan for each and every marriage. He brings us together for a specific purpose. We can ask God to show us *why* he called us to serve him in marriage and for *what* purpose he intends to use us. Our goal is eternal life in heaven. We must help each other get there. Because of human nature, we will naturally give each other opportunities to practice forgiveness. We shouldn't stop at what comes naturally, but rise to the supernatural, stretch our spiritual muscles, grow in virtue, and encourage one another in what is right and true. As faithful companions on the journey, we experience the joy of two hearts aligned in love with a shared purpose and goal.

**Prayer:** Lord, not our will, but your will be done today. Not our plan, but your plan do we desire to pursue. Please give us the grace we need to live the life you have planned for us. Amen.

# Day 311

*The life of the body is the soul; the Life of the soul is God.*

— *St. Augustine of Hippo*

Just as God breathes life into our bodies and his spirit into our souls, so too does he breathe his life and spirit into our marriage if we allow him. Since we have free will, we must invite God into our marriage and cultivate his spirit through daily prayer as a couple. He needs our mutual "yes;" not "maybe," not "when we have time," not "on our terms," but a wholehearted *yes* to allow the Holy Spirit to move freely and fully in our marriage. Our marriage is authentically alive when the Holy Spirit is flowing through it and guiding our life together. It is in this way that we walk together, hearts united, toward our eternal home.

**Prayer:** Lord, please daily breathe your Spirit into our marriage so we may continually walk in your will. Amen.

# Day 312

*And now, O Lord, I am not taking this sister of mine*
*because of lust, but with sincerity. Grant that I may*
*find mercy and grow old together with her.*

*— Tobit 8:7*

Here Tobit prayerfully proclaims that he marries not for selfish physical pleasure, but for genuine and pure motives. Were our reasons for marrying our spouse genuine and pure? How have our initial motives affected our marriage, positively or negatively? As husband and wife, we are ordained by our Lord to respect, support, and mutually uphold one another until death. When we love each other in this way into old age, we are setting in order God's divine plan for marriage from the beginning.

**Prayer:** Lord, purify our motives. Make us sincere in our love, that we may uphold each other into old age. Amen.

# DAY 313

*It is not enough for us to say, "I love God."*
*But I also have to love my neighbor.*

— *St. Teresa of Calcutta*

Spouses love one another deeply, but they don't always find each other lovable. Sometimes, we need to ask God to fill in the gaps where our love for our spouse is lacking. It is in these moments that we must remind ourselves that God loves our spouse more than we can, even more than we can comprehend. The love we have for our spouse is meant to reflect the love God has for us. Married couples are called to be living, breathing images of the love God has for his people. This is the ideal we aspire to live; it is the summit God places before us to climb together as married.

**Prayer:** Lord, where our love for one another falls short, please fill in the gaps with your love. Keep us aware of how much you love each one of us. Amen.

# Day 314

*Don't allow any sadness to dwell in your soul, for*
*sadness prevents the Holy Spirit from acting freely.*

— *St. Pio of Pietrelcina*

Though it is human to feel sad from time to time, surrendering to sadness prevents love itself from acting freely in our life. Sadness can begin small but grow like a cancer. If left unchecked, it can color everything and steal our hope. It is good to bring our sadness to God in prayer and ask for the grace we need to dismiss it from our souls. The unconditional love of the Holy Spirit can overcome all adversity and bring us hope, inspiration, and strength, both individually and in our marriages.

**Prayer:** Lord, when we are tempted to let sadness dwell in us, renew our joy. Amen.

# Day 315

*Your way of acting should be different from the world's way.*

— *St. Benedict of Nursia*

The ways of the world contradict the precepts of God and his original plan from the beginning. As Christians, we are called to live in the world, but not of the world. From time to time, we all struggle with one or more of the seven deadly sins: pride, greed, lust, envy, gluttony, wrath, and sloth. Saint Benedict urges us to recognize the false "happiness" earthly pleasures only temporarily afford, and the shallowness of a life based on worldly standards. Instead, he encourages us to strive for the Christian virtues, particularly chastity, temperance, charity, diligence, patience, kindness, and humility. How are these virtues manifested in our marriage? Do we guard our souls from pornography so we can wholly and purely love our spouse? Are we patient with our spouse or do we get irritable and cranky? Do we humbly recognize that our gifts and blessings come from God, or do we flaunt our achievements? A respectable and happy marriage consists of two imperfect people who both daily strive for virtue.

**Prayer:** Lord, help us to live in the world, but not of the world. Amen.

# DAY 316

*There is no saint without a past, no sinner without a future.*

*— Attributed to St. Augustine of Hippo*

Saint Augustine embodied these words. His life as a young man was characterized by loose living and a constant search for answers to life's basic questions. He enjoyed the ladies, drinking, and carousing. But he underwent a major conversion and is now recognized as one of the greatest saints of the Church. Augustine reminds us that we are all sinners and not one of us is perfect. Wherever we are on our spiritual journey, we can find hope in the fact that we are not alone in our struggles. God will give us the strength to overcome them. Take heart that all marriages struggle from time to time. What we see on the surface of "ideal" marriages is only a partial picture of their daily lived reality. There are good and solid marriages, no doubt! However, many of these "good" marriages have a past, and many "not-so-good" marriages have a future.

**Prayer:** Lord, thank you for reminding us that, although we are sinners, we are called to overcome our weaknesses by your grace. Amen.

# DAY 317

*Remember that when you leave this earth, you can take with you nothing that you have received, but only what you have given: a full heart, enriched by honest service, love, sacrifice, and courage.*

*— Attributed to St. Francis of Assisi*

There is nothing wrong with material wealth, provided it does not become an idol. When God blesses us financially, he expects us to use our wealth in a way that honors him. When we pass from this world to the next, our legacy will not be our material and worldly gains but how well we lived the Christian virtues. This life is intended to prepare us for eternal life. If we have not willingly sacrificed, deeply loved, or served our spouse, family, and others, then our hearts will be empty. The more fully and purely we live the vocation of marriage here on earth, the more prepared we will be for the wedding feast of heaven.

**Prayer:** Lord, thank you for all your blessings. Help us to live our marital vocation each day with our end goal of heaven in mind. Amen.

# DAY 318

*But God shows his love for us in that while*
*we were yet sinners Christ died for us.*

— *Romans 5:8*

God is Love — true, unconditional love and not the worldly fast-food version of love the media tries to make us believe will bring us happiness. It's no wonder that loving him is the greatest romance! The most tangible way we experience the love of God and engage in this beautiful and holy romance is through the love we share with our spouse in marriage. This is where God's love is made real and where we are given the opportunity to find him every day.

**Prayer:** Lord, thank you for allowing us to engage in the greatest romance ever through the love we have for one another which flows from you. Amen.

# DAY 319

*It is not hard to serve when we love that which is commanded.*

— *St. Ignatius of Loyola (quoting Saint Leo)*

Today, the word "obey" has a meaning significantly different from its origin. To obey implies a level of control with an associated penalty for not obeying. For example, we must obey traffic signals; and if we don't and get caught, then a police officer will hand us a ticket. So, to whom does Saint Ignatius refer, and how does obedience apply to marriage? The word "obey" comes from the Latin *obedire*, literally meaning: "to lend oneself in the direction of what or whom you hear." So, what Saint Ignatius is really saying is: "It is not hard to lend ourselves in the direction of whom we hear when we love the one whom we hear." Interesting, isn't it? This is true to our experience. When we love the one who's talking to us, we want to obey that person. If we love and reveal that love to our spouse, then we will respect, admire, and be open to our spouse's guidance.

**Prayer:** Lord, help us to respect one another and love each other enough to lend ourselves in their direction. Amen.

# DAY 320

*One earns Paradise with one's daily task.*

— *St. Gianna Beretta Molla*

We hear this common rally in business, sports, and life all the time: "Just keeping going, you can do it — one step at a time!" When you really stop to think about it, isn't life just one long, never-ending pep talk? Roadblock after roadblock, challenge after challenge, issue after issue, the choice we have is to forge ahead or give up. The same is true of marriage. Marriage is difficult at times. Think about all the little tasks we have to do as husbands and wives. While salvation is a free gift we cannot really earn, our daily tasks in marriage, done for love, pave our way to heaven.

**Prayer:** Lord, show us how to grow closer to eternal life in paradise with you, one faithful task at a time. Amen.

# Day 321

*You can't give God deadlines.*

— *St. Pio of Pietrelcina*

God is never early, never late, but always on time. It's just that we aren't patient! When we find ourselves in a difficult situation in marriage, it may be tempting to give God a deadline for when we want the tide to turn. While it is good to talk to God and lay before him what weighs on our heart, we must not expect him to work within our timeframe. God works outside of time, in his own powerful and mysterious way. Some of the deepest struggles in our marriage have turned out to be blessings in disguise. In the moment, we could have never seen nor comprehended what God was doing. In retrospect, we have been able to see how he was working all things for the good of our marriage. God's timing is perfect.

**Prayer:** Lord, please help us trust in your perfect plan and timing in all aspects of our lives. Amen.

# Day 322

*For truly, I say to you, if you have faith as a grain of mustard seed, you will say to this mountain, "Move from here to there," and it will move; and nothing will be impossible to you.*

— *Matthew 17:20*

A volunteer at Maria's new workplace suggested that her nephew and Maria should meet. There was one complication, though: James lived on the east coast, and Maria lived in Minnesota. After many long late-night conversations, they quickly gathered how much they had in common. Their deep family roots, appreciation for older things, and mutual love of the Catholic Faith drew them together, so they decided to officially meet in person. James flew to the snowy Midwest for their first in-person date. By the time he left, Maria had booked a flight to see him and meet his family. Long-distance relationships aren't easy. Throughout the challenging times, they both relied on the hope that God had a plan for their lives together. With each trial overcome and each milestone met, their love for one another grew deeper, and their conviction in God's will for their future together increased. Maria and James now live within minutes of each other and eagerly look forward to their life together united in marriage.

**Prayer:** Lord, give us the faith to move mountains. Help us to remember that with you, nothing is impossible. Amen.

# Day 323

*Perseverance in little things for love is heroism.*

— *St. Josemaría Escrivá*

In order to stay emotionally connected with our spouse, we need to persevere throughout the day. Are we emotionally available when our spouse attempts to connect, or do we act as if we are listening when in reality we are disengaged? The most successful marriages are those where both husband and wife have an awareness of their spouse's desire to connect, and they respond in love with open ears and open hearts. Keep trying to connect even when it's hard. Take an interest in what your beloved shares with you, and persevere. Ask questions and follow up later by referring back to something they previously shared. Don't simply exist date night to date night or vacation to vacation, but thrive in your marriage through intentional connection every day.

**Prayer:** Lord, increase our awareness of the moments we try to connect and help us to persevere in acting on our desire to remain connected to each other. Amen.

# DAY 324

*In a true marriage, there is an ever-enchanting romance.*

— *Ven. Fulton J. Sheen*

With the exception of an anniversary or special occasion, romance often fades within the first few years of marriage. When the reality and expectations of day-to-day life set in, romantic love can seem like a distant memory. And yet, romance is an essential element of a healthy and vibrant marriage. Within the context of a pure and committed marital relationship, romance can enrich the marriage and increase the enjoyment of married love as God intends. However, romance for the sole sake of romance can be destructive. Feasting on romance novels, chick flicks, and sexually themed television shows can set us up with unrealistic expectations. We must love one another passionately and be intentional about keeping romance alive in marriage, using creativity to fashion romantic moments. Each love story is a beautiful mosaic composed of millions of moments.

**Prayer:** Lord, show us how to experience our marriage as "an ever-enchanting romance." Amen.

# Day 325

*How sweet is your love, my sister, my bride!*
*how much better is your love than wine,*
*and the fragrance of your oils than any spice!*

*— Song of Solomon 4:10*

The Song of Solomon is a conversation between two lovers — King Solomon and his beautiful Shulamite bride. It is a poem that celebrates the voices of two lovers as they praise one another and longingly yearn to be one. King Solomon says that the love he holds for his bride is not only "sweet," but has the profound respect and appreciation a brother would have for his sister. To him, her love is better than wine and her fragrance is more attractive than perfume. It may be difficult to keep this kind of love burning inside us for the rest of our lives, but most of us can recall the intoxicating power of love as we once perceived it. We are drawn to union by the sweetness of the beloved.

**Prayer:** Lord, help us to remember the sweetness of our love and the beauty of the union to which you have called us. Amen.

# Day 326

*Enjoy life with the wife whom you love, all the
days of your vain life which he has given you under
the sun, because that is your portion in life and
in your toil at which you toil under the sun.*

— *Ecclesiastes 9:9*

To enjoy means to live *in* joy. Etymologically, though, the root of *enjoy* carries a much deeper meaning. Where today we might say: "Enjoy your meal" or "Enjoy Spring Break," the word was intended to mean something closer to "May you rejoice in …" (fill in the blank). Put in that context: to rejoice in marriage and family life is a far cry from just having carefree fun. It is to be delighted, amazed, and abundantly joyful! Still, life is tough and can be downright miserable. Yet the Book of Ecclesiastes reminds us that it is our vocation — indeed our godly calling — to rejoice in our spouse through the arduous toils of daily life.

**Prayer:** Lord, teach us to enjoy the life you have given us and to rejoice in one another. Amen.

# Day 327

*When Joseph woke from sleep, he did as the angel
of the Lord commanded him; he took his wife.*

— *Matthew 1:24*

As an ordained Catholic priest shepherds his flock and is ultimately responsible for nurturing the souls of his parishioners, a married man is the spiritual head of his home and shares a similar responsibility for members of his family. God calls men to die daily to themselves and to strive to live selflessly. Their most important role and purpose is to help their wife and children get to heaven. God gives us the ideal example in the Holy Family. The Holy Family's prayerful obedience to God's will is the *true* model for us, and that obedience *is* attainable! With God's help and lots of prayer (and coffee!), Troy strives to live for our family as Saint Joseph did for his. While he is aware of his shortcomings, Troy praises God each day that he has another chance to fulfill God's mission for him on earth.

**Prayer:** Lord, please help us model our family after your family. Help us to be a holy family. Amen.

# DAY 328

*In like manner this applies to those also who are in*
*great fear, for they are so intent on their own passion,*
*that they pay no attention to the suffering of others.*

— *St. Thomas Aquinas*

When we fly in a plane, we have the advantage of looking at life below us from a different perspective. Everything looks smaller, but we can see the bigger picture. Troy remembers flying over the Caribbean Sea to the island of St. Lucia. Since the water was so clear, he could see abundant life below the surface of the shallow water. It was spectacular! But if he had seen it at ground level, his view and impression would have been much different. Sometimes we need to take a step back in life and view things from a different vantage point. Fear often arises from the inability to see below the surface to what truly is going on. As a spouse, it is our duty to strive to understand our husband or wife. That is when compassion flows naturally. We drive out fear when we choose to sympathize and share their pain. We all act unlovable at times, and we usually need love the most when we deserve it the least.

**Prayer**: Lord, when fear enters our hearts, remove it and replace it with your peace. Help us to see below the surface to your abundant life in us. Amen.

# DAY 329

*Love lives through sacrifice.*

— *St. Maximillian Kolbe*

St. Maximillian Kolbe neither says nor implies that love *lived* or *will live* by sacrifice, but rather he very explicitly states that love *lives* by sacrifice. Used in the present tense, the action is clearly ongoing and without end. Love happens in this very moment, the moment of sacrifice. In his mystical wisdom, Kolbe implies that love cannot live without sacrifice. Therefore, sacrifice is our means to keep loving even when the world, our bodies, and our temperaments tell us not to or that it's no longer worth it. And since the ultimate sacrifice was given by Christ himself, we can turn to him to learn how to love unconditionally.

**Prayer:** Lord, please give us the grace to live the words, "Love lives by sacrifice," in our marriage. Amen.

# DAY 330

*Love bears all things, believes all things,*
*hopes all things, endures all things.*

*— 1 Corinthians 13:7*

Hope and conviction are the oxygen that fuels the fire of endurance. When we believe God has a plan and purpose for all things that he allows in our marriage, we can press on during challenging seasons. When a marital problem weighs us down, we can fall prey to speaking ill of our spouse to others. Our pain spills over into our conversations and before we know it, we are complaining about our spouse and how difficult it is to love him or her. Saint Paul tells us that "love bears all things." Married couples must protect the sacredness of their union by quietly bearing the load through the grace of our sacrament. If it is a serious matter, then seek counsel or choose one faithful person to confide in. We must speak well of our spouse and showcase their strengths, not their weaknesses or faults. Let love for our spouse shine through the way we speak about them when they are not around.

**Prayer:** Lord, give us the grace we need to bear all things, believe all things, hope all things, and endure all things in love. Amen.

# Day 331

*I will not allow myself to be so absorbed in the*
*whirlwind of work as to forget about God.*

— *St. Maria Faustina Kowalska*

Work is at the service of the family. We don't live to work; we work so we can truly live. While we may enjoy our jobs, they must never take us away from God, but rather draw us toward him. We can make use of sacramentals such as a scapular, a rosary, holy water, a crucifix, or a prayer card as tangible ways to remind us of God's presence in our life. As men or women of faith in the workplace, we should always keep our faith with us throughout the day. Troy had a college roommate who used to put a prayer card right in front of him while he typed at the computer as a reminder that there is a higher purpose than simply completing a deliverable. To this day his example stands out. What can we do to better protect our souls in the workplace?

**Prayer:** Lord, may we never become so absorbed in the whirlwind of work that we lose sight of you and your plan for our lives. Amen.

# DAY 332

*Be subject to one another out of reverence for Christ. Wives,*
*be subject to your husbands, as to the Lord. For the husband*
*is the head of the wife as Christ is the head of the Church.*

*— Ephesians 5:21–23*

Many people think this verse is archaic and anti-feminist and are immediately repulsed by it. But this verse is designed to draw us into the depth, beauty, and sacredness of marriage. To be "subject to" means to be under the mission of. When a wife is subject to her husband, she is under his mission. This means that men must get their mission right. Wives may be subject to us, but we are subject to God. Our mission is to get our wife and family to heaven by daily laying down our life in a total gift of self. When a husband does not fulfill his role according to God's design for marriage, then the wife often steps into his role out of perceived necessity. Consequently, the marriage and family become disordered, and chaos results. But when a husband steps up to the plate and fulfills his role as head of the household faithfully, his wife can have confidence in their mutual mission and in his leadership. The natural order of headship God intends in marriage then flows freely.

**Prayer:** Lord, help us each fulfill our roles as husband and wife according to your design for marriage. Amen.

# DAY 333

*Give thanks in all circumstances; for this is
the will of God in Christ Jesus for you.*

*— 1 Thessalonians 5:18*

"Gratitude is attitude." We've all heard the catchy cliché. Yet how often do we *really* live it? Saint Ambrose elevates the act of showing thanks to the level of an urgent duty. The concept of giving thanks appears frequently in the Bible. There, the word "thanks" conveys an outpouring of praise to God both for who he is and what he has done. Imagine how different the world would be if more of us truly believed that returning thanks was an urgent duty, not just to God but to other people. We can begin that transformation at home by thanking our spouse, not just when we get around to it, but with urgency.

**Prayer:** Lord, thank you for our marriage and all we do for each other every day. Amen.

# Day 334

*Do not grieve over the temptations you suffer. When
the Lord intends to bestow a particular virtue on us, he
often permits us first to be tempted by the opposite vice.
Therefore, look upon every temptation as an invitation
to grow in a particular virtue and a promise by God
that you will be successful, if only you stand fast.*

— *St. Philip Neri*

Every one of us yields to temptation from time to time, it's part of our fallen human nature. But we need not lose hope. When we are tempted to sin, we can ask God to show us which virtue he is offering us. One practical action we both do is an examination of conscience at the end of the day. We take inventory of the good and the ugly from our day, and offer to God both our thanksgiving for his grace and our plan for how to do better next time in resisting the temptations that caused us to fall.

**Prayer:** Lord, when we are tempted to sin, give us the grace to grow in the opposing virtue. Amen.

# DAY 335

*For with God nothing will be impossible.*

*— Luke 1:37*

Since marriage is our vocation, it is our way of life and our path to holiness. Any time is the perfect time to do a sort of marriage inventory. Is our marriage bringing us closer to Christ? Are we loving each other with God's love or simply trudging along, trying to make it on our own? In order to love the way God loves, we need to know God. The only way to know God is to spend time with him. We don't have to do anything fancy. Just pick a form of prayer that we are both comfortable with and that is realistic to commit to. Decide to grow closer to God as a couple, and tend to the things that need some extra tender loving care. When we do what we must, we will begin to do what we can. Suddenly, we will find ourselves doing things we never imagined we could.

**Prayer:** Lord, refresh our love and help us to grow closer to you. Amen.

# DAY 336

*Prayer is to our soul what rain is to the soil.*
*Fertilize the soil ever so richly, it will remain*
*barren unless fed by frequent rains.*

— *St. John Vianney*

We both enjoy gardening as a hobby, so we can appreciate the importance of frequently watering and fertilizing the soil to nourish crop growth. The smaller the plant, the less established the root system is, and the more frequently we need to water it. A larger plant has a more established root system and can go for longer stretches without water. When it comes to prayer, the deeper our relationship with Christ is, the more natural it becomes to make prayer an integral part of our day. We hunger for time alone with God and cultivate patience as we wait on God in prayer. In marriage, we must also "water" our love frequently and "fertilize" it often if we expect it to grow and mature. The deeper marital love grows, the greater desire we both have for moments to further water and fertilize our marriage.

**Prayer:** Lord, show us how to make time together a priority so our marriage can flourish. Amen.

# Day 337

*With all my heart I repent of ever having offended you. Grant that I may love you always; and then do with me as you will.*

— *St. Alphonsus Liguori*

Beyond Sunday Mass, it is good to take advantage of the numerous spiritual opportunities offered throughout the liturgical year to grow in holiness as a married couple, and more deeply surrender to God's will. The Advent season begins the liturgical year and is a perfect time to prepare our hearts together to receive Christ more fully at Christmas. During Lent, praying the Stations of the Cross together at home or with your parish community is a beautiful way to enter into the mystery of the cross as a married couple. Throughout Ordinary Time there are several opportunities to enhance our relationship with Christ, including Bible studies, ministries, and charitable service. Pick a few faithful and enlightening podcasts to listen to, read a spiritually uplifting book, go on a retreat, watch an inspirational film, or follow inspiring Catholics on social media. Taking advantage of these resources can help strengthen our faith and marriage.

**Prayer:** Lord, lead us to the resources that will help us grow closer to you and in deeper understanding and appreciation of the Church's teachings. Amen.

# DAY 338

*When a man loves a woman, he has to become worthy of her. The higher her virtue, the more noble her character, the more devoted she is to truth, justice, goodness, the more a man has to aspire to be worthy of her. The history of civilization could actually be written in terms of the level of its women.*

— *Ven. Fulton J. Sheen*

We've all heard the maxim "Behind every great man is a great woman," but how often have we stopped to think about what it really means? Sheen rightfully proposes that the viabilty, stamina, and maturation of society reflects the caliber, intellectual prowess, virtues, and moral character of its women. A man's productivity and virtue waxes and accelerates when his professional and personal bar is raised by a woman he loves. The higher the moral bar is raised for the gentleman to earn the right to her heart, the more he has to work for her, and the more he must become to win and keep her.

**Prayer:** Lord, show us how to raise the bar for each other, not to discourage, but to elevate. Amen.

# DAY 339

*Therefore a man leaves his father and his mother*
*and clings to his wife, and they become one flesh.*

*— Genesis 2:24*

When two become one, the challenge often presents itself, *which one?* In all seriousness, blending two lives into one is both beautiful and painful. Anything we do for our spouse, we essentially do for ourselves. It is not my house or your house, it is our house. It is not his problem or her problem, it is our problem. It is not his success or her success, it is our success. We are called to share virtually everything in order to live marriage according to God's plan. This does not mean that we lose our individual identities, or we are unable to take credit or responsibility for successes and failures, but rather we share the mental load of all of life's ups and downs together, united in the Sacrament of Matrimony.

**Prayer:** Lord, help us continually blend our two lives into one each day by dying to our own selfish wants for the greater good of our marriage. Amen.

# Day 340

*We must not forget that only when love between human*
*beings is put to the test can its true value be seen.*

*— Pope St. John Paul II*

While no one will ever live the full meaning of love as God defines it, it is our duty to try. And if anything worth doing is worth doing well, then striving to live one's life with love must also be done well. Loving rightly is no easy matter. To love a spouse means to be patient with him or her when mistakes, sometimes serious ones, are made. It means to die to our own selfish desires when we know that our selfless act will spiritually benefit our spouse, even when our sacrifice comes at the most inopportune time. Maybe we turn off the ballgame with only a minute left to play and our favorite team's outcome hanging in suspense just to make a late-night run to the grocery store that can't wait till tomorrow. Or maybe we're readying to soak in the tub after a long day when a glass is shattered and needs to be cleaned up. Like fire to precious metal, each little adversity we encounter shows us the true value of our marriage and helps us grow stronger, as long as Christ is at the center.

**Prayer:** Lord, please help our marriage grow stronger through each test we encounter. Amen.

# Day 341

*There is still time for endurance, time for patience, time for healing, time for change. Have you slipped? Rise up. Have you sinned? Cease. Do not stand among sinners but leap aside.*

— *St. Basil the Great*

One night during the Christmas season, Kathleen was sitting on the couch cuddling our son when she noticed the train encircling the bottom of our Christmas tree had come off the track — a common occurrence with a toddler in the house. She thought about how easy it is to get off-track in life, especially in our walk with God and in our marriage. Despite how much work or how tedious it might be to get our "train" back on track, we need to put the effort in if we desire to make spiritual progress and have a healthy and holy marriage. All married couples fall off the track from time to time. What's important is getting back on track and being a conduit of mercy to facilitate the process. When our spouse has slipped, forgive, even when it's not deserved. Practice mercy when we'd rather cast stones. Show love even when we feel betrayed. For the spouse who has fallen, humbly receive the mercy extended. Utilize the grace of the Sacrament of Reconciliation, along with your marital grace, to begin again.

**Prayer:** Lord, in the moments we get derailed, please help us realign ourselves through the gifts of your love and mercy. Amen.

# Day 342

*We shall steer safely through every storm so long*
*as our heart is right, our intention fervent, our*
*courage steadfast, and our trust fixed on God.*

— *St. Francis de Sales*

Lynne, the godmother to our youngest child, recently vacationed in St. Lucia. Lynne and her husband stayed at a place perched high on the side of a mountain overlooking a bay. Lynne soon realized that she had a bird's eye view. The people in the bay could only see as far as the horizon allowed them, but she could see when the storms were rolling in. With each storm, Lynne saw that with the use of proper instruments available to monitor the weather, the people below might have avoided the storm all together and enjoyed nicer weather a few miles down the island. Similarly, if we use the instruments that God offers to live a joyful life in line with his will, there are many storms that we avoid. When we follow the Ten Commandments, live the Beatitudes, and adhere to the teachings of the Catholic Church, we are less likely to find ourselves engulfed. How frustrating God must be, watching us endure tough storms in our marriage, when we could have avoided them if we had used the instruments he's given us.

**Prayer:** Lord, help us clearly see the big picture of our lives and use the tools you give us to steer clear of the avoidable storms. Amen.

# DAY 343

*Every moment comes to us pregnant with a command*
*from God, only to pass on and plunge into eternity,*
*there to remain forever what we have made of it.*

— *St. Francis de Sales*

If you talk to anyone who has lost their spouse suddenly, the common theme is the desire for one more day, one more moment, one more kiss, one more embrace. We do not know the day or hour we will be called home, but we do know that the present moment is a gift. As married persons, do we value the moments we have with our spouse, or do we waste the gift of time we have been given? Sadly, it is often not until we come face to face with the reality that life is fragile, that we realize the preciousness of each moment. But we can always choose to turn the television off, put our phone down, or come home from work early one day. Let's make the most of the time we have with our beloved, creating life-giving memories that bear fruit.

**Prayer:** Lord, help us be present to one another and value the moments we have together. Amen.

# DAY 344

*Be angry but do not sin; do not let the sun go down on
your anger, and give no opportunity to the devil.*

— *Ephesians 4:26–27*

Feeling angry is normal, but when we let anger build inside of us instead of expressing the emotion in a healthy manner, we poison our relationships. Anger left to fester builds in intensity. Like something under extreme pressure, it expands until it cannot be held back anymore, often bursting in a volatile display of emotion. Something we could easily discuss and deal with today has the potential to turn into a significant conflict a few months down the road, after the anger has had time to grow. Unresolved anger becomes corrosive over time and gives the devil an opportunity to step in and turn our hearts against our beloved.

When anger arrives on the scene, set time aside as soon as possible to sit down together and work through the conflict. Once emotions have calmed down and are under control, we can lovingly communicate our feelings and what made us angry. Make it a habit to deal with anger when it comes to keep it from turning into resentment or toxic behavior.

**Prayer:** Lord, please help us deal with anger and conflict in a healthy and mature manner. Amen.

# DAY 345

*This is my body which is given for you.*

*— Luke 22:19*

The summit of the Mass is the Eucharist, and the pinnacle of marriage is the consummation of two bodies as they become one. In the first, Christ sacrificially offers his body for all of humanity for the forgiveness of sins. In the second, husband and wife each give their bodies freely to one another in the marital embrace. Both acts give life. The Eucharist brings spiritual and eternal life to the communicant, while marital consummation has the power to bring forth children. Our bodies belong to our spouse. Do we withhold sexual intimacy from our spouse as a means of control or punishment? Sex is holy and is meant to be a sincere gift of ourselves, even when we are not in the mood, even if we feel like our spouse does not deserve it, even if we are hurt or angry. The marital act, when given in love, has the power to heal and restore.

**Prayer:** Lord, please provide us the grace necessary to continually, lovingly, and willingly offer our bodies as gift to one another. Amen.

# Day 346

*Prayer is the remedy when temptations to sin rage in the heart.*
*Whenever you are tempted to sin, pray, and pray earnestly.*
*Frequent prayer renders powerless the assaults of vice.*

— *St. Isidore of Seville*

Life is full of temptations that can steal our peace; therefore, it is essential to arm ourselves with prayer. The greatest weapon of defense against temptation is frequent prayer. The more we pray, the more we are spiritually equipped to resist temptation and the wiser we become in avoiding situations that may cause us to sin. At times, we will be tempted to be lazy in showing love for our spouse. It doesn't take much experience to realize that our spouse will not always act in ways that motivate us to love them. In fact, many times their behavior will make it harder to love. But love is a decision we make over and over again and put into action through the grace of our sacrament. Often, it will be challenging to find the inspiration to express love for our spouse. This is natural even in the healthiest of marriages. When our love for God is the reason for loving our spouse, then our love, is guaranteed.

**Prayer:** Lord, keep our desire to love one another rooted in our love for you. Amen.

# DAY 347

*An action of small value performed with much*
*love of God is far more excellent than one of a*
*higher virtue, done with less love of God.*

— *St. Francis de Sales*

A few years into our marriage Troy began leaving little rolled up love notes between two kitchen-cabinet handles every few weeks. He continues to perform this simple act of love now, years later, and Kathleen always looks forward to finding his notes. This repeated small act of love has taken on incredible value in our marriage over the years. Our children also look forward to discovering daddy's love notes to mommy. When children witness their parents love for one another, they feel assured and secure. At one point in time, our middle son also left Kathleen cute little love notes on a different cabinet for a period of about a year. It was precious and a prime example of how children model what they see. It only takes one small pebble to create a ripple effect in water, and it only takes one small act of love to create a ripple in our marriage. Never underestimate the value of an action done with authentic love for your spouse.

**Prayer:** Lord, help us never underestimate the eternal value of an action done with authentic love. Amen.

# DAY 348

*Be patient with everyone but especially with yourself;*
*I mean that you should not be troubled about*
*your imperfections and that you should always*
*have courage to pick yourself up afterwards.*

— *St. Francis de Sales*

Sadly, it is common for one spouse to place a guilt trip on the other when a hurtful behavior has left them wounded. We should not let their words and actions push us to give way to discouragement, despite whatever we did or did not do to cause them pain. Instead, we can recognize our sin, apologize, and then have patience with ourselves. Our faults do not define us; they are merely evidence that we are sinners like everyone else. We are all created in God's divine image and in need of God's ocean of mercy.

On the other hand, if we have been wounded by our spouse, we should not attempt to make him or her feel guilty. Rather, we can express our concern and hurt in a mature and loving manner. Then ask God to help our spouse come to the realization of their sinful behavior on their own. We should offer our spouse the freedom to confess and move forward in love.

**Prayer:** Lord, help us have patience with ourselves and with one another, while always recognizing our value in you. Amen.

# Day 349

*As gifts increase in you, let your humility grow, for you*
*must consider that everything is given to you on loan.*

— *St. Pio of Pietrelcina*

No matter how talented, smart, fast, creative, inspiring, or productive we may be today or become tomorrow, God authors it all. He facilitates, fertilizes, and nurtures our growth like the landowner does his vineyard. The more he blesses us, the more he expects of us. A few years ago, Troy received a prestigious, hard-earned award from his employer. He was the North American MVP for a global software company's Project Management Office. When his award was made public, Troy used his platform to honor God and our marriage. He publicly stated that behind every good man is a good woman, and most importantly he gave all glory to God for his achievement. The humility Troy displayed when he was given a large platform left an impression on Kathleen's heart.

Each gift we are given is to be used for God's glory. We should avoid comparing our accomplishments or our marriage to others. Pride inflates the ego. Humility helps us take our place gracefully and utilize our talents wisely and with purpose.

**Prayer:** Lord, we recognize that all we are and all we have are gifts from you. Help us to faithfully and humbly use the talents you have given us to glorify you. Amen.

# DAY 350

*The virtue of patience is the one which*
*most assures us of perfection.*

— *St. Francis de Sales*

When long-married couples are asked the recipe for marital success, many identify patience as a key ingredient. Patience within marriage means differentiating between what needs to be changed and what ought to be tolerated. We must choose our battles wisely and learn to accept certain behaviors and personal characteristics. Some behaviors need to be challenged for the personal growth of the individual and the good of the marriage. If one spouse is irresponsible with money management, then this strains the marriage and needs to be discussed lovingly and calmly at a time when both spouses are well rested and can focus on the issue at hand. In addition to being patient with one another, couples need to be patient with their marriage. Healthy marriages grow and change over time. All couples go through periods of disenchantment and monotony. Although challenging, this is normal and requires patience to work through, in order to emerge into the next season with a greater appreciation of one another.

**Prayer:** Lord, please help us be patient with ourselves and with one another and discern between what needs to be changed and what must be tolerated. Amen.

# Day 351

*Few human joys are as deep and thrilling as those
experienced by two people who love one another and have
achieved something as the result of a great shared effort.*

— *Pope Francis*

Every year, just the two of us get away for a few days — though at times, we have brought along a nursing baby. There are always several obstacles to work through, including hiring a babysitter. We often question whether it is worth all the effort and financial investment. But after every trip, we have come back refreshed and grateful that we did make the effort to strengthen our marriage, renew our love, and create some fantastic memories! Escaping as a couple alone for a few days might not be a feasible reality. What's most important is that we do set time aside to invest in our marriage. Go on a date night. Have a romantic meal at home after the children go to bed. Take a walk. Spend a night at a local hotel. Do something fun together! Whatever works for you and your unique situation and season. It's worth the effort.

**Prayer:** Lord, we desire a great marriage, and we know that requires work. Assist us and guide us each day as we put in the effort to achieve a dynamic, healthy, and holy marriage. Amen.

# DAY 352

*The way of a fool is right in his own eyes,*
*but a wise man listens to advice.*

*— Proverbs 12:15*

It is prudent to seek advice from individuals who have successfully walked the road before us. When it comes to marriage, gleaning wisdom from faithful couples who have "been there and done that" can save us years of heartache. God intends for us all to grow and learn from one another. Painful lessons can often be avoided through discovering those same pearls of truth from a married couple who have grown in wisdom through their own successes and failures. To avoid common pitfalls in marriage and support continual positive growth, it is important for a husband and wife to pursue godly advice from experienced mentors.

Wherever you are on your journey, never stop seeking wisdom to grow in your vocation. Also, be willing to share the wisdom you have gained with other married couples. We are all in this together as the Body of Christ.

**Prayer**: Lord, please provide us with married couples that we can learn and grow from through their wisdom and example. Amen.

# DAY 353

*He who finds a wife finds a good thing,*
*and obtains favor from the LORD.*

— *Proverbs 18:22*

Just before we married, Kathleen's dear, sweet mother pulled Troy aside and said, "Kathleen's got a heart of gold! Life together won't be perfect, but her heart will always be in the right place." We had known each other since college, so Troy had some idea of what she meant. But he could not have imagined the fuller extent until many years later.

We have endured our share of disagreements and hardships. We have a child with special needs, lost three children to miscarriage, one to an ectopic pregnancy, and another to SIDS. We took Kathleen's mother into our home at the end of her life so she could enjoy her last days with us, and survived two separate cancer scares which — by the grace of God — turned out to be benign. Through it all, the words Kathleen's mother spoke to Troy have been proven true. He who finds a good wife indeed obtains favor from the Lord.

**Prayer:** Lord, may our marriage always honor you through all of life's ups and downs. Amen.

# Day 354

*And a voice came from heaven, "You are my*
*beloved Son; with you I am well pleased."*

*— Mark 1:11*

It is important to recognize our husband or wife's accomplishments, big and small, and let them know when we are proud of them. Compliment them on a project completed. Let them know how delicious the meal they cooked was. Tell them how nice they look, or what a good parent they are. Whatever it is that we are proud of in our spouse, we should make sure they know it. Complimenting our spouse is not meant to be approached as a one-and-done proposition or something we do once in a while. It should be ongoing. Call attention to the qualities we love and cherish and do it frequently. We should also seek opportunities to honor our spouse publicly by showing our appreciation in the presence of others.

**Prayer:** Lord, help us to affirm each other and openly express the pride we take in one another's accomplishments. Amen.

# DAY 355

*For I was hungry and you gave me food, I was thirsty and you gave me a drink, I was a stranger and you welcomed me.*

*— Matthew 25:35*

Marriage is a calling to genuine servanthood through faithfulness each day in caring for our spouse and their unique and individual needs. Do we take an interest in our spouse? Do we pay attention when they talk and ask questions to learn more? We should be attentive to our spouse's needs, rather than expecting them to meet our needs. It may be simply bringing your husband a glass of water while he is working, or ensuring the car has gas in it for the next time your wife drives. The more attentive we are to our spouse's needs, the more we are equipped to anticipate their needs. For example, Kathleen likes our bedroom warm and cozy when we go to bed, so every night Troy turns our space heater on a few hours before we turn in. It's a simple gesture, but it communicates love because he not only anticipates her need, but takes the time to meet it. This is authentic love.

**Prayer:** Lord, help us to be attentive to one another's needs each day and serve each other in authentic love. Amen

# DAY 356

*But the LORD said to Samuel, "Do not look on his appearance or on the height of his stature, because I have rejected him; for the LORD sees not as man sees; Man looks on the outward appearance, but the LORD looks on the heart."*

— *1 Samuel 16:7*

How different life would be if our culture promoted interior beauty, the kind that never fades, but rather increases through the years. We are quickly approaching our fifties. Our bodies have been showing signs that we are not the youthful couple we once were. Growing old is not a process we gave much thought to until recently. We were busy having babies and raising a family. In some ways it sneaked up on us. But we're discovering a new joy we didn't expect.

Unfortunately, we live in a disposable culture. Most things are not built to last, and we don't even want things to last, lest we lose out on the latest and greatest. It can be tempting to transfer this same mentality to marriage. If we rely on the physical appearance of our spouse to motivate us to love, our "love" will be tested when their appearance changes. Authentic love appreciates exterior beauty, but is drawn in through interior beauty, which becomes more attractive with age.

**Prayer:** Lord, as we grow older together, help us to grow in greater appreciation of one another and more deeply in love. Amen.

# DAY 357

*Do not be deceived: "Bad company ruins good morals."*
*Come to your right mind, and sin no more.*

— *1 Corinthians 15:33*

A few years ago, we spent a decent amount of time with two married couples from our parish. We had children of similar ages and we all got along well, but morally we were not aligned on many levels. Keeping up with the demands of friendships that were not overall healthy for our marriage took time and energy. For a while, we felt like God wanted us in their lives to evangelize; and candidly, we both enjoyed their company and the upscale parties they hosted. However, through a series of events, it became clear that God was asking us to pull back. We only have so much time, therefore it is wise to invest time into friendships that share our values and encourage us in our vocation of marriage.

Choose your company carefully to avoid occasions of sin. Sometimes that can even mean certain family members. Put healthy and holy hedges around your marriage to keep outside negative influences at bay.

**Prayer:** Lord, please bless us with wholesome friendships that challenge and encourage us as a couple to grow in holiness. Amen.

# Day 358

*Do you want to have God always in your mind? Be
just as he made you to be. Do not go seeking another
you. Do not make yourself otherwise than he made
you. Then you will always have God in mind.*

— *St. Anthony of Padua*

We should never pretend to be someone we're not, even if we feel like it might win our spouse's affection in the moment. Authenticity is attractive. If our spouse does not value who we really are, then they are the one missing out, not us. But sometimes we struggle to accept ourselves. Jesus is our hope, and our self-worth is found in him alone. When we look for our identity or worth elsewhere, we are left feeling empty. We must let our souls discover our true worth in the God who created us. Then together, we will venture on a new journey of mutual self-discovery and acceptance.

**Prayer:** Lord, show us how to seek our worth in you alone. Help us to fully accept who we are, and who we can be, in you. Amen.

# DAY 359

*Let him seek God in all things and in all places,*
*and he will always find Him at his side.*

— *St. Peter Claver*

Everywhere we look, we can see God in some form. Whether it is in the delicate flower in full bloom, the sound of a songbird, the smile of a child, or the homeless man on the street. God is present all around us if we look at life through eyes of faith. Sadly, the place we ought to seek him most, the heart of our spouse, is a place we often overlook. Over time, married couples can become blinded by hurt and shame, and fail to see God alive in their spouse as a result. In sacramental marriage, a husband and wife are called to be Christ to one another. The love of God is intended to be manifested through the exchange of marital love, and in this way married couples always find God by their side.

**Prayer:** Lord, may your love continually be manifested in our marriage through our love for one another. Amen.

# DAY 360

*If we do not carry our crosses with joy*
*then they will be of no use to us.*

— *St. John Vianney*

We often think the crosses we are asked to carry are so much heavier than those carried by our friends, siblings, or even our spouse. When that's the case, we often get annoyed when our husband or wife complains about their sufferings instead of showing them compassion and sharing the burden. While we all have a different capacity for pain, we must never diminish the pain our spouse is in, but rather do all we can to help them carry the cross they have been given. All crosses have value when we offer the suffering to God. We can waste our pain, or give it to God for a specific intention. When spouses help one another carry their crosses, they both receive the benefit of offering up the suffering for a greater good, which in turn strengthens the marital bond.

**Prayer:** Lord, we offer up our suffering this day for our marriage. Help us to grow and blossom according to your plan. Amen.

# DAY 361

*Everything, even sweeping, scraping vegetables,*
*weeding a garden and waiting on the sick could*
*be a prayer, if it were offered to God.*

— *St. Martin de Porres*

Each day, we are given an opportunity to sow seeds of love through the little things we do to live our vocation of marriage. These seeds eventually produce a bountiful harvest. Couples often make the mistake of searching for the "large ticket items" in marriage to get more bang for their buck, more return on their investment. This causes them to underestimate the incredible value of doing the next good thing in front of them. Giving a gift, planning a romantic evening out, or turning on our charm often carry less value in the eyes of our spouse than pouring our love into the mundane, necessary tasks each day. Real love is found in the everyday details. Ordinary things, when offered to God, are prayer.

**Prayer:** Lord, help us sow seeds of love each day through faithfulness to the details of our vocation. Amen.

# DAY 362

*For whoever would save his life will lose it; and whoever*
*loses his life for my sake and the gospel's will save it.*

— *Mark 8:35*

Not one of us can avoid the death of our physical body, but there is another kind of death, which paradoxically cultivates life. It is dying to our own selfish desires and sins each day so Christ can more fully live in us. When we decrease, Christ can increase. Death to ourselves is the barometer of our life in Christ. In marriage, the more we die to ourselves, the more our marriage grows and thrives. It is a paradox of love. When we say no to a night out with friends and yes to an evening home together, our marital love grows. When we say yes to physical intimacy despite not being in "the mood," our marital love grows. When we stop what we are doing to truly listen and enter into what our spouse is sharing, our marital love grows. Initially the growth is incremental, but it becomes substantial over time as we die more and more to ourselves.

**Prayer:** Lord, please help us die daily to ourselves so our marriage can thrive in your love. Amen.

# Day 363

*Charm is deceitful, and beauty is vain,*
*but a woman who fears the LORD is to be praised.*

*— Proverbs 31:30*

During Kathleen's junior year in college, she studied abroad in Gaming, Austria, at a former eighteenth-century Carthusian monastery. The women's dorm rooms were on the top floor of the monastery, and at the bottom of the stairs was a large mirror. It was common for all the young ladies to stop and take a peek at themselves in that mirror every day on their way to class. One day, Kathleen went to take a quick glance at herself in the mirror, but the mirror was gone. In its place was a large poster that read, "Charm is deceitful, and beauty is vain, but a woman who fears the Lord is to be praised." This change of décor made a significant impact! Our interior beauty is far more valuable than our exterior beauty. It is godly to make ourselves attractive for our spouse, but interior beauty should be our focus.

**Prayer:** Lord, help us continually develop the richness of our interior life so we may become more attractive to one another with each passing year. Amen.

# Day 364

*When he saw the crowds, he had compassion for them, because they were harassed and helpless, like sheep without a shepherd.*

— *Matthew 9:36*

Jesus recognized that the crowd was mentally and physically depleted, and although he was probably exhausted himself, he offered words of encouragement to them. We should never overlook our spouse's fatigue or play it off as if it is simply part of their job description instead of looking for ways to help ease their burden. There are times when we are drained on every level and devoid of sufficient sleep. That's when we should treat each other gently. We often underestimate the detrimental and ripple effects of exhaustion. When we don't get enough rest, we are not able to properly think, reason, or love. Couples should take what they can off their plates so they can each take care of their physical, spiritual, and mental needs, as well as the health of their marriage.

**Prayer:** Lord, please help us to take care of our health so we can be at our best for you and for one another. Amen.

# Day 365

*The glory ... of the Lord's passion ... is chiefly*
*wonderful for its mystery of humility, which*
*has both ransomed and instructed us all.*

— *St. Leo the Great*

As husband and wife, we are called to model Christ in our marriage with all our heart, soul, and mind, despite all our human weaknesses, inadequacies, and baggage. Jesus is the perfect example. He shows us the way, but we still must be open to it. When we are closed, our guard goes up, and we kick into protectionism and selfishness. We see ourselves as the focal point (even if we don't admit it) and wonder how we could ever be wrong. We become the opposite of humble. But when we enter marital union and strive with God's help to see our spouse and the world in humility, we experience salvation. The greatest toil in marriage is our journey toward holiness. We make that journey best on our knees.

**Prayer:** Lord, we come to you in humility and ask that you help us die to our selfishness to live our vocation of marriage in a way that leads us both to heaven. Amen.

# ACKNOWLEDGMENTS

Thank you to our friends and family who mentored us along our journey and encouraged us to share our story and lessons learned. Your support and prayers kept us moving forward in faith despite the intense spiritual warfare that surrounded the writing of this book.

Special thank you to the couples who contributed their personal marriage stories used in this book.

# About the Authors

Troy and Kathleen Billings met at the University of Notre Dame when paired up to perform a dance together for a Christmas show. Several years later their lives reunited, and they fell in love, thus beginning their real dance together in the Sacrament of Marriage. In 2020 they relocated from a suburb of Chicago to Greenville, South Carolina, with their five children, ages eight to twenty-five. They also have four children in heaven. Troy is a multilingual corporate global business executive, and Kathleen has a BA in Theology from Franciscan University of Steubenville, which she leverages as a national speaker and author. Kathleen writes for Catholic Mom and WINE (Women in the New Evangelization). She is a contributing author to *Amazing Grace for Mothers* (Ascension Press) and *Called by Name: 365 Daily Devotions for Catholic Women* (Ave Maria Press).

Troy and Kathleen created a vibrant, parish-based marriage ministry called BAM: Building Amazing Marriages, which they directed from 2010 until 2020. Shortly after moving to South Carolina, they began hosting a monthly family Rosary and dinner at their five-acre homestead, which attracts between 250 and 300 people per month. They also developed and co-lead weekend marriage retreats and marriage days of renewal called "Simply Love." Troy and Kathleen have a blog entitled *Two to Tango* in the "For Your Marriage" section of the United States Conference of Catholic Bishops (USCCB) website, and are frequent guest speakers nationwide on marriage and family life. To invite them to speak at your parish or host a marriage retreat or marriage day of renewal, email Kathleen at seasonsoftheheartandhome@gmail.com.